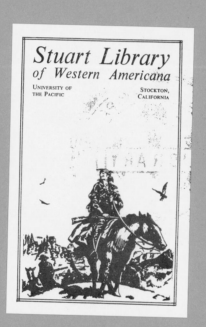

Growing Up on Bald Hill Creek

HARVEY M. SLETTEN is a free-lance writer and a lifelong resident of North Dakota.

Growing Up on

Bald Hill Creek

Harvey M. Sletten

Iowa State University Press/Ames

HARVEY M. SLETTEN, a native North Dakotan, received the B.S. degree from the University of North Dakota and the M.A. degree from Purdue University. After a career of public school teaching, he has turned to writing. His articles and poems have appeared in *North Dakota Journal of Education, North Dakota Outdoors, Evangelical Beacon, War Cry, Air Progress, Capper's Weekly, Michiana, In Retrospect* (NDRTA), and *Good Old Days.*

© 1977 The Iowa State University Press
Ames, Iowa 50010. All rights reserved

Composed and printed by
The Iowa State University Press

First edition, 1977

Library of Congress Cataloging in Publication Data

Sletten, Harvey M   1912–
    Growing up on Bald Hill Creek.

    1. Sletten, Harvey M   1912–
2. Hannaford, N.D.—Biography. 3. Hannaford,
N.D.—History. I. Title.
F644.H36S587   978.4′34   [B]   77-23848
ISBN 0-8138-0080-3

Contents

In Gratitude

*For every still strengthening memory
of this story's heroine,
my ninety-three-year-old mother, Amelia Sletten.
Her own youthful dreams of becoming a schoolteacher
were sacrificed
when she assumed the responsibility of caring
for younger brothers and sisters
at the tender age of fifteen.
She was determined that her children would get an education.*

Prologue

In the small towns of America, before the land
filled up, life was free, uncluttered and filled
with hope.

—ROD MACLEISH
"National Spirit: The Pendulum Begins to Swing"
Smithsonian, July 1976

MY father and mother were both born in Minnesota. Father, followed by his brother Albert and two sisters, moved to North Dakota in the early 1900s. They all settled down in the vicinity of Hannaford, a small though bustling town in east central North Dakota. They were a part of the second boom in that state. North Dakota experienced a tremendous surge in railroad building from 1898 to 1915. Branch lines zigzagged across the treeless prairie in a veritable network. The railroad companies saw fit to establish stations every five or six miles. Along with the small boxlike shack that served as a depot would often go loading pens or stockyards for the cattle shipper. One or more grain elevators for wheat storage and shipment would soon follow. In this way a profusion of new towns were born, springing up everywhere like toadstools in a rain forest. If a town appeared before the railroad entered the region, it often moved to a location on the railroad when the line came through. The new towns, even small ones, quickly acquired many business and professional enterprises. Perhaps a general store would appear first, to be followed by blacksmith shop, livery stable, and saloon. Eventually the town would boast a bank or two, hotel and boarding house, lumberyard, drugstore, a doctor, churches, a school, and perhaps even a newspaper.

Each town saw itself becoming a thriving metropolis replete with all the refinements. Neighboring towns vied with each other

"Proving up" homestead claim shack. Grandma and Grandpa Rasmussen (with stovepipe hat). 1887.

Carl and Amelia Sletten, married 1909.

Hannaford, shortly after 1900. Presbyterian church on the left, Lutheran church on the right.

Road-building crew west of Hannaford in 1914.

The train depot at Dazey, nine miles south of Hannaford.

for the farmer's business and community spirit often led to intense rivalry.

Hannaford was first served by a branch line of the Northern Pacific Railroad coming out of Valley City. In 1912, the Great Northern inaugurated service on the Surrey Cutoff, which ran from Fargo to Surrey, a station just east of Minot. Hannaford happened to lie on the route too, and so had the distinction of being served by two railroads.

My father came hoping to share in the expected growth. He and his brother Albert were carpenters by trade and found ready employment during the boom period. With hopes for an optimistic future, Father courted and won my mother's heart in 1909. Their first child, the Obie of this story, was born in 1910. I came into the picture in 1912.

From recollection and record I will relate some of the memorable episodes in the life of a lad growing up on Bald Hill Creek, a rather insignificant part of the Red River of the North Drainage Basin. Waters of the Bald Hill flow into the Sheyenne River just north of Valley City. The Sheyenne in turn empties into the Red River a few miles north of Fargo. Since the Red River flows northward into Canada, water from tiny Bald Hill Creek eventually finds its way to Hudson Bay. Hannaford could have been Any Small Town, U.S.A., at a time when America was still very rural in its habits and thinking. I trust this very personal story of a typical family growing up in rural America during the period from about 1918 to 1932 will bring you a pleasant touch of the past. If you are an older reader, perhaps it will provide a nostalgic return to scenes of your own childhood. In all probability, you can identify with every history-making event and empathize with the happiness and heartache alike. If you are young, try to believe that grandpa and grandma were once kids like you. This was their generation—the "kicking over the traces" 1920s and the desperate 1930s. Your grandparents may have experienced hardships quite unreal to you, but to them the American Dream was real and dear. They were optimists of the first order and were endowed with a powerful sense of being special in the eye and intent of God.

HARVEY SLETTEN

Fort Ransom, North Dakota
June 1977

Growing Up on Bald Hill Creek

1

Mother Caught a Bullhead

THE first warm days in May we would start to pester Mother to let us go swimming. She had an inflexible rule: when the leaves of the poplar reached the size of a silver dollar, it was time to go swimming—not before. This relationship was always a mystery to us, but we knew better than to argue. To impatient lads, those leaves took their own sweet time in growing. Lacking a silver dollar to use for comparing we would bring in carefully selected specimens for Mother to judge. A silver dollar in those days, the early 1920s, was a mighty big coin—no doubt about that. Finally Mother decided that an ample outer limit of leaf area had been reached. She had her next year's credibility to protect.

Our faded cotton bathing suits had long been ready. There had been the annual trying on for size, with a downward switching from oldest to youngest of the four boys. Last summer's tears had been mended and the seams reinforced. Bathing suits of that period were one piece and skirted over the attached pants. Cotton bathing suits had a tendency to cling when wet, but nonetheless were insisted upon by mothers. "Skinny-dipping," though frowned upon, was only indulged in in such out-of-the-way places as Ferris's slough.

Our swimming hole was a natural one, a beauty, on Bald Hill Creek. This happy little stream meandered just below the sleepy little town where we lived. The Nile River in Africa has been called the "Father of Egypt." To boys growing up in Hannaford, Bald Hill Creek was foster-mother, nursemaid, and Dutch uncle, all rolled into one. Its crowning glory, without a doubt, was the swimming hole.

At just the right place below the town, the often shallow and narrow stream obligingly widened and deepened. On one side a six- or seven-foot-high bank provided a challenging takeoff for cannonball jumps and high dives into water perhaps eight or nine feet deep. The bottom dropped off quite abruptly. On the opposite side the depth tapered off to an exposed sandbar.

Most boys in Hannaford had learned to swim by the time they were six or seven years old. There was no instructor and no lifeguard on duty. The neophyte swimmer dog-paddled around in the shallows with one foot on the bottom until ready for the initial attempt to negotiate deeper water. Then he took off for the sandbar, arms and legs churning. Never-to-be-forgotten elation was his when exploring toes felt the security of solid bottom. From then on progress was rapid. More sophisticated strokes were practiced and diving and underwater swimming were added to the repertoire.

I do not recall any drownings in Hannaford, though youngsters literally "grew up" along the creek. Hannaford mothers were a courageous lot, and I'm sure they prayed. Also, at that time there were few household conveniences to lighten the work load of busy mothers. Life was grim and hard, and in some respects the creek, with all its fascinations for growing boys, may have been a blessing. At least it kept the youngsters from underfoot.

Our family did have a profound scare on one occasion. My youngest brother, affectionately called "Bumpy," had received Mother's permission to go to the creek to swim. On his way to the swimming hole he was accosted by our Uncle Lefty and Bill Brown. Uncle Lefty had heard that my brothers and I had recently caught some fine northern pike somewhere along the creek. He asked Bumpy if he knew where. Bumpy explained that this particular fishing place was not easy to direct anyone to, but avowed that he was available and could take them there. "Jump in," said Uncle Lefty and off the three chugged in the Model T.

This was early afternoon. Suppertime came—and no Bumpy. My father sent us out to search. We could find no trace of Bumpy. The swimming hole was deserted, and no one along the way had seen him. By now my parents were definitely worried. Father contacted our town marshall, who decided to organize a search. The fire bell at the village hall was sounded to summon searchers. As preparations were being made to drag the swimming hole, Uncle Lefty, Bill Brown, and Bumpy drove into town. By now it was almost dark. They seemed surprised at the furor they had caused. With the fish biting and a "jug" to share, time was the least concern of Uncle Lefty and Bill Brown. It was some time before Uncle Lefty dared come to our house again.

Fishing the Bald Hill occupied almost as much of our time as swimming. Equipment was simple. A ten- or twelve-foot cane pole might cost from fifteen to thirty-five cents. A good-sized hank of heavy linen line took another dime. A single-shank hook and a medium-sized cork at a penny each generally completed the gear. A feathered spoon hook at twenty-five cents was a longed-for luxury and marked its proud owner as the "compleat" and sophisticated angler.

Stringing a cane pole properly was an art in itself. One end of the linen line was fastened securely several feet below the tip of the pole. This was a safety precaution in case the thin tip section of the bamboo pole should break while landing a heavy fish. A half hitch was then made just below each node, moving upward toward the tip. The line was secured firmly again at the tip and then measured out to extend a couple feet beyond the butt end of the pole. If the line was too much longer than the pole, the outfit became unwieldy and difficult to swing and drop the hook where wanted.

It was not much out of the way to go past the butcher shop on our way to the creek. We were usually able to con butcher "Stub" Johnson out of some beef scraps to use for bait. Sometimes these were retrieved from the sawdust-covered floor around his cutting block. If Stub was in a good mood from imbibing vanilla extract, we might even get a chunk of tough neck beef. A bit of that on the hook would keep "nibblers" from stealing the bait. An extra bargain might be struck with Stub if he needed an errand boy. Entrusting his young accomplice with half a dollar, Stub would send him to the Mercantile store for a bottle of vanilla extract. "If they ask whom it is for, tell them, 'my mother,' " Stub cautioned.

I quit going after a suspicious clerk inquired, "You're sure it isn't for Butch Johnson?" National prohibition, declared in effect in January 1920, had failed to alter the personal habits of the likes of Stub Johnson. A pocketful of cookies from a bulk bin was the customary reward from Stub for a mission completed. Such a snack on a fishing trip was a temptation hard to resist.

There was a practical side to our fishing expeditions. The fish we caught augmented Mother's limited food budget. Perhaps this was why we could occasionally wangle a quarter for a new pole or a dime for a new line. In a way, I suppose, it was a capital investment.

Father was a laboring man and worked hard six days a week. Sunday was his only day of rest. Nonetheless, if we coaxed hard enough, he would often forego his afternoon nap and walk with us along the creek as we fished. Sometimes the fishing hole we had in mind was a mile or more distant, arrived at by following devious paths known only to young adventurers. Father plodded doggedly along in the rear. Now and then, pausing for breath, he would hopefully suggest, "Boys, this looks like a good place. Why don't you try it here?"

Seldom, however, could we be dissuaded from our appointed destination. We didn't hold it against Father, however, for trying. As we neared our rendezvous, where the big ones lurked, the pace quickened. "C'mon, Pa, we're almost there! It's just around the bend."

"Uh huh, that's good. Go on ahead—I'll catch you."

Even before we stopped, lines were being unwound and the poles readied. Hooks were hurriedly baited, each of us vying to be the first to wet his line. Often, by the time Father arrived, the first fish was already flopping on the bank. Invariably Father's first concern was to find a shaded spot where he could stretch out. His snores did little to disturb the quiet hum of a summer afternoon on the Bald Hill. The red-winged blackbird swaying on bended cattail cocked its head in Father's direction but scarcely paused its melodious trill. Four intent boys, eyes glued to bobbing corks, themselves were strangely quiet—"all nature seemed in rhyme."

Only rarely did Mother succumb to our enticement and join us on a fishing safari. Part of her reluctance may have been because skirts were ill fitted to the tortuous paths we followed through bramble and thistle patch alike. One such memorable occasion stands out. Perhaps with the thought that Mother's resolute courage in accompanying us that day should be rewarded, Obie thrust his fishing pole into her hands. Shortly her cork bobbed a couple of times, then sank out of sight.

"Mother, you have a bite! Pull in! Pull in!"

As Mother lifted the line a squirming bullhead came into view. To the uninitiated, a bullhead presents a rather frightening appearance with its large head and gaping mouth adorned with tentaclelike appendages. Mother let out a shriek and threw bamboo pole and all into the water. Thereafter we glumly decided that fishing probably wasn't her forte. But, oh how she could fry the fish! And that was pretty important, too. The bullhead incident merely confirmed her role and perhaps even enhanced her stature in our eyes.

Shiner fishing was a variation of our fishing pursuits. Shiners, chubs, and redfins or redhorses abounded in the shallower stretches of Bald Hill Creek. These minnowlike species do not reach any appreciable size, most running in a three- to perhaps seven-inch range. Occasionally a granddaddy chub or redhorse that had escaped being prey for larger fish might reach a magnificent nine or ten inches in length. These fish were edible, though their small size made cleaning them a tedious chore. They were also bony.

We fished them either to use for bait for larger fish or for the sheer sport of catching and releasing them. A five- or six-foot pole, a bit of line, and a tiny barbed hook was all that was needed for tackle. In a pinch, even a bent straight pin would serve as a hook. Often the tip end of a broken bamboo pole, or a willow shoot growing straight and slender and limber enough to offer a little play, made the perfect shiner pole. A small grasshopper impaled on the point of the wee hook offered a tempting mouthful to a voracious chub or shiner. The larger redhorse often lurked beneath the overhang of an exposed rock. It took a little maneuvering to float a grasshopper toward such a rock and have the current suck it down into the shadows. A slight tug, telegraphed through line and pole to eager arm, signaled that mister redhorse had inhaled the hopper. A triumphant grin split sunburned face as the plump little fish was lifted from his watery hideaway.

Shiner fishing often developed into a contest to see who could catch the most. Each contestant did his own tallying and it was not unusual to hear such scores called out: "I have forty-one."

"That's number fifty for me."

"Forty-seven comin' up!"

Most of the time the winner's count was accepted. Another day would be coming. Only "Baaba" Larson's claims were suspect. We learned that the only way Baaba could be bested was for one of us to delay his final tally until after Baaba had announced.

Wild berry picking along the Bald Hill seemed to go hand in hand with fishing. In our never-ending search for new fishing

holes, we stumbled upon the berry troves. Juneberries were usually the first in season. These mouth-watering delights were not too
plentiful, however. Some summers they weren't to be found at all.
Late spring frosts may have had something to do with the unpredictable yields of the juneberries. When we did find them in
quantity, our family could look forward to a rare table treat.
Mother would delve into her reserve coin jar and find fifteen cents
to spend for cream.

Ordinarily the quart of whole milk we bought each day from
the Willses was let stand overnight in a pan for the cream to rise.
Mother would then skim off the cream as best she could with a
large spoon. She garnered just enough cream from the quart of
milk so that used sparingly, it was enough for her own and
Father's coffee needs.

Knowing that juneberries in cream was to be our supper
dessert, there was no dearth of volunteers to fetch the cream.
Clutching the covered glass jar containing the precious nickel and
dime, one of us would speed his barefoot way to the Wills home.
The Willses lived only about half a block down and across the
street from us and they kept a few cows.

When juneberries were at their best, some were almost as big
and blue and delicious as today's commercially grown blueberries.
Mother sometimes ventured a juneberry pie, though usually any
excess beyond the juneberry and cream treat was preserved as
juneberry sauce. The jars were stored on the wooden shelves that
lined our cool, earth-walled cellar.

Wild strawberries came about midsummer, but never
abounded. Sweet and delicious, they were usually consumed as
picked—on the spot. We searched for these tasty red morsels on
hands and knees. The discoverers of a wild strawberry patch
endeavored to keep its whereabouts secret as long as possible. My
older brother, Obie, and his inseparable pal, Ole Thorseth,
managed to keep their choice find a private preserve summer after
summer. If interlopers attempted to follow, and goodness knows
how many times we tried, Obie and Ole would lead us on a wild
goose chase. We could only guess at the extent of their treasure.
Judging by the small tin pail of surplus that Obie occasionally
brought home to share, we imagined a meadowful. We knew the
berries brought home to be overflow because Obie would
generously decline his supper portion of wild strawberries and
cream.

Chokecherries were usually ripe and ready to pick by late
summer. Gathering them was a family enterprise. The best

Del, Harvey, and friend Leo with a catch of shiners, chubs, and red-horse from Bald Hill Creek.

Bumpy, age eight, 1925, modeling cotton, skirted bathing suit.

chokecherry spots were several miles distant and usually the family car was pressed into service. Our first and only family car was of pre–World War I vintage. It was an open model Chevrolet. The cloth top had been taken off and a wetting from a sudden summer rain shower was always a possibility. Since we had no shed for the car, it stood in the backyard quite exposed to both the elements and the assaults of young make-believe drivers. It took some readying if a trip were planned. In fact, preparing the car became a major undertaking for Father. Usually at least one flat tire had to be repaired. The engine had to be hand-cranked, and after standing for days unused, it invariably balked. Father spent a lot of time either peering under the hood or crawling underneath the car itself. We boys learned that it was discreet to view Father's shakedown operation from a remote vantage point.

On one such occasion, Father had worked all Sunday morning on the automobile. About noon he came into the house, covered with grease from head to foot, and triumphantly announced that the car was all set to go. A short time later, as we were eating our Sunday dinner—all keyed up with the exciting prospect of an afternoon automobile ride—we heard a loud "bang" in the backyard. No one said a word, but we covertly watched Father's neck redden, and he almost strangled on his soup. The bang was unmistakable. A tire had let go—blown out. Mother tried to save the day: "It's really too hot to go riding anyway."

The chokecherry expedition was planned for a day when Father did not have to work. Mother would prepare a picnic lunch and we'd try to get an early morning start. This was contingent, however, on Father's success with the car. Breakfast was scarcely eaten before we youngsters had piled into the back seat. Only after the engine sputtered into life would Mother condescend to clamber into the front seat. With an air of expectancy we watched Father make last minute adjustments of his cap and goggles. Fortunately, Father always announced our departure: "Everybody set? Hang on—here we go!"

We had learned to be wary of Father's lurching starts. He never did master that tricky clutch pedal.

Over deeply rutted, rocky trails we chugged and bumped along. Pasture gates had to be opened and closed, and Obie struggled manfully with those. Now and then we would jolt over a hidden badger hole and startled, Father would exclaim, "What was that?"

With exaggerated sweetness Mother might reply, "That? oh that was only an abandoned well."

When an almost imperceptible trail ended or became impassable, we would pile out, take our lunch and pails, and continue our journey on foot. Often this meant crossing the creek by stepping from stone to stone. If anyone wet his feet, it was usually Father. Mother proved surprisingly nimble.

Soon we were all stripping the clusters of ripened chokecherries. Each picked at his own apportioned level. Father could usually manage all but the very highest clusters, and sometimes even those branches could be bent into reach. While Bumpy's range was limited, he picked and ate until the tart chokecherries made his tongue too wooly to swallow more. Wild chokecherries were mostly pit, with only a thin fleshy layer between pit and skin. We would pop several into the mouth at once, then pits were spat out in staccato bursts. When pressed between thumb and forefinger, the moist and slippery pit became a stealthy projectile to launch at an unsuspecting cherry picker. By tacit understanding, Father was a forbidden target.

Once Bumpy reached the "wooly mouth" stage, his attention was easily diverted to other pastimes. A garter snake slithering its way through the grass would quicken its darting movements when stirred by an eager Bumpy in pursuit. Or a fat and lazy grasshopper might wind up a captured victim after a well-executed stalk. Bumpy had to learn that Mother was less than enthusiastic when the hapless insect spit "tobacco juice."

By late afternoon we usually had our quota of chokecherries. We had paused earlier to enjoy a leisurely picnic lunch. Father would swing the filled, hundred-pound flour sack of chokecherries to a broad shoulder and we would start the trek back to the car. One particular hurdle remained for Father—crossing the creek on the stones. The load on Father's shoulder made him even less agile. About halfway across, what we expected to happen invariably did. Father's exploring foot would light either on a wobbly rock or on one that was wet, moss covered, and slippery. For a moment Father and load would teeter precariously, then, rocks abandoned, he would lunge the last several steps through often knee-deep water. We boys could scarce hide our amusement, while I know Mother let out a sigh of relief.

There was still the perilous ride home to anticipate, but at least we had negotiated the creek. Eventually we would arrive back home—tired but content.

For Mother, work with the chokecherries was only beginning.

They were washed by dumping into a water-filled tub. Leaves, bugs, and other foreign material floated to the top and were removed. Next the chokecherries were cooked in a large kettle. This process would release much of the juice. Then the remaining pulp, mostly pits and skins, was put into a cloth bag or enfolded in a flour sack dishtowel. Draining and no end of vigorous hand squeezing extracted most of the remaining juice. Mother's hands would bear the dark red stains for some days after.

Quarts and quarts of chokecherry juice were canned and stored on the bulging cellar shelves. Later, the juice would be converted into jelly or syrup as needed. Chokecherry syrup on pancakes was delicious, and we even poured it atop our steaming bowls of oatmeal. Mother may have overdone it. To this day I can scarcely look a bowl of oatmeal in the eye. If Mother didn't invent "back to nature" cereal, she certainly popularized it in our household.

A part of the bounteous chokecherry harvest became the makings for chokecherry wine. A batch was "set" in a five-gallon stone crock which occupied a niche beside the pantry cupboard. A dish towel was draped over the crock to keep out flies and to partly conceal the operation from curious eyes. A "revenooer" would only have needed to follow his nose to the cache. The fermenting chokecherries had a sour-mash odor all their own.

One day Mother had removed the cover—perhaps for wine tasting. Obie passed by, proudly bearing a small frosting-covered cake. Somehow his prized cake slipped off the plate and plopped into the open wine crock. For some time after, Delbert and I made the most of Obie's chagrin. We rubbed salt in his wound by joining in a nonsensical ditty, "Down went McGinty to the bottom of the sea."

Mother's chokecherry wine served a double purpose. I'm certain that she and Father enjoyed a wee nip of it on special occasions. Mother also served up a thimble-sized glass of it to any of us showing symptoms of a winter cold. We found it to be quite pleasant medicine. One year there were no chokecherries and Mother made dandelion wine instead. That winter, Obie opined that it was hardly worth getting sick anymore.

2

"Y'er Out!"

ALL during the early 1900s, Hannaford was noted as a good baseball town. Baseball fever affected young and old alike. The main focus, of course, was on the "town" team or the "big" team. Competition with surrounding towns was intense, and to bolster local talent, Hannaford usually imported a hired battery.

Sunday afternoon baseball was an institution throughout the summer months. Occasional weekday games were scheduled for early evening, usually at 6 o'clock or 6:30. This meant an early supper and a scramble to get to the ball park. The townspeople turned out en masse to watch the hotly contested games. Local pride often led to foolhardy wagers. The park had neither grandstand nor bleachers, and spectators either sat in automobiles or on the ground. Two eight-foot-high chicken wire wings extended from the fenced backstop out beyond first and third bases to give token protection to windshields. It proved well-nigh impossible to keep eager youngsters and overly exuberant adults behind this woven-wire barrier and officials made only a half-hearted attempt.

There was never a dearth of shaggers for the foul balls. Not every errant ball was recovered. Some landed in adjacent weed patches or bounced into adjoining yards to disappear in garden or shrubbery. These "lost" balls did not go unnoticed by observant small fry. We marked well the vanishing site for later covert search and retrieval. Such alertness provided the baseballs for backyard playing catch, as well as for almost daily skirmishes on a nearby vacant lot.

Hannaford's baseball team had its heroes for ardent young admirers. Custer Stafne could hit the ball a country mile. His towering home runs often cleared a row of scraggly trees that crossed deep center field. Also "Cus" could really fly on the base paths. By the time the opposing fielder had reached the ball, Cus had streaked across home plate. His cigar-smoking brother, "J. B.," played first base and batted left-handed. J. B. was a terrific clutch-hitter and we "oohed" and "ahed" at his vicious line drives to right field. Jack Rierson was a mainstay of dependability in the outfield. When Jack thumped his glove, the crowd knew the fly ball would "fall in a well." Jack, however, wasn't too speedy afoot, and a long fly ball over his head spelled trouble. His lumbering pursuit gave the hitter ample time to circle the bases.

Two nonplaying townsmen shared both the spotlight and the player-hero role. Shorty Twitchell and Hank Ferris were the two most active as well as the most vocal of all Hannaford fans. Their antics were a delight to the eye and in critical moments of a game provided the spark that would ignite a rally.

Shorty was our local barber. His five-foot figure was a constant fixture along the third base line. The raucous voice emanating from this diminutive man caused more than one opposing pitcher to either walk a batter or throw a wild pitch past the catcher. Umpires were almost certain targets of Shorty's wrath. He would show his displeasure at an unfavorable call by charging onto the playing field and vigorously kicking dirt in the offender's general direction. This added emphasis to the verbal abuse of which Shorty was a master.

Hank Ferrris was a slow-moving mountain of a man. During a game he stationed his imposing bulk along the first base side of the diamond. A cigar was always clamped between his teeth. While Hank lacked Shorty's volatile style, his very size intimidated anyone inclined to argue. Hank had one other claim to fame. His 280-pound bulk had anchored down the back seat of an Essex automobile on a wagered, timed run from Hannaford to Fargo. With Hank in the rear for ballast, the ninety-odd miles over graveled roads had been negotiated in less than two hours. That record stood for some time.

One umpire in the area could not be fazed by either Shorty's antics or Hank's menacing scowl. Stub Skow made his decisions fearlessly and with finality. His "Ye'r out" reverberated across the diamond and the up and outward sweep of his arm was irreversible. Shorty once tried to cajole Stub into changing a close call. Hannaford's second baseman, George Peterson, had been ruled out sliding into third base. The game was a close one and George protested he was safe, claiming that he hadn't been tagged. Stub, as usual, was adamant, and desperation prompted Shorty to intercede. "Now, Stub, you know that George is a deacon of the church. If he says he was safe, you have to take him at his word."

"I don't care if he is St. Peter himself—he's out!"

The argument was over.

Traveling baseball teams were occasionally booked and always drew large crowds. Often such teams were composed of talented black ball players and invariably they would beat Hannaford handily. With such names as Union Giants or Kansas City Monarchs emblazoned on their uniforms, we regarded these traveling professionals with awe-struck wonder and admiration. It seemed as if our vaunted Hannaford heroes fully expected to get beat. One of these black teams had a pitcher named John Donaldson, whose fame as a strike-out artist preceded the team wherever it played. Talk was that Donaldson might have been good enough to pitch in the major leagues had he been a white man.

Donaldson wasn't in the lineup the day the Giants played Hannaford. I don't suppose they used him in every game. Along about the seventh inning, with Hannaford trailing by a nine-to- one score, the crowd started to chant, "We want John Donaldson! We want John Donaldson!"

One of his teammates informed the fans that "Big Jawn" was cleaning carbon. Sure enough, in a nearby clump of trees where the visitors had parked their cars in the shade, John Donaldson was working on an engine. The tall, lanky figure was clad in coveralls and he wiped grease from his hands as he ambled in to the pitcher's mound. He obliged the fans by striking out hard-swinging Jack Rierson on three straight pitches. "Big Jawn" acknowledged the applause of the crowd by doffing his battered cap, then went back to cleaning spark plugs.

Another traveling team called themselves House of David. We often wondered whether they actually had any affiliation with the religious organization of that name. At any rate, all of these players wore long hair and beards. They, too, were quite skilled and put on a good show, including a pregame "pepper game." During one of these games Custer Stafne sent one of his towering drives toward the trees in left center field. That ball had home run written all over it, but with long hair streaming, the House of David center fielder raced back and made a leaping one-handed catch of the ball from amid the very tree branches. As the story of this fantastic catch was later related, it received some embellishment. The generally accepted version had the bearded outfielder bend the tree aside with one hand while he casually reached up and speared the ball with the other. A somewhat less credible account had him climb the tree to make the catch. Cus could only lament, "I wuz robbed!"

Obie and Bumpy aspired to be catchers and strove mightily to

Bumpy aspired to be a catcher. 1925.

Tina, age four, 1925, in the barren yard. Father's car is in the background.

improve their backstopping. I was a pitcher and Delbert a somewhat indifferent fielder. We encouraged our "baby" sister Tina to chase the ball for us when frequent wild throws sent it rolling into Mother's garden or bouncing across the road. She wasn't too dependable as a ball shagger, however, her enthusiasm for the job waning about the time we were just getting warmed up. A high, fast one might sail over Obie's head and he would holler, "Tina, will you get the ball? Tina? Tina? Now, where did she go?"

Obie would go after the ball with an air of injured resignation. "Girls! No wonder you don't find 'em on baseball teams! Humph!" Returning to his station behind our designated home plate, Obie would fire the ball back at me and bark, "Now throw a few over the plate for a change!" He would set up a target for me with his pood. (Kids in those days referred to the catcher's mitt as a pood.) My pitches didn't hit the outstretched pood too often, and that may have been why Obie preferred to catch for his pal, Ole.

Our yard seemed to be a natural rendezvous for all the kids in the neighborhood, or, I know Father thought, for the whole town. After a few abortive attempts, Mother and he had wisely abandoned any hope of growing a lawn. Father's car and a sturdy swing had their alloted places next to Mother's garden. Battered horseshoe stakes peeked above deeply worn pits next to neighbor Jackson's tree hedge. Obie's babbitt foundry with its rock-circled fire pit and blackened melting pan occupied a corner next to the horseshoe pits. The rest of the yard was scarred with well-worn paths between pitcher's mounds and makeshift home plates (layout of the diamond changed, depending on wind direction and number of players). There were also jumping pits, a shotput ring, and pole vaulting standards. Interspersed throughout were apt to be old wheels, boards, worn-out bicycle tires, and countless other treasures scavenged from city dump and neighbors' trash piles alike. If the clutter became too offensive to Father's eye, or if he stumbled over things when crossing the yard after dark, a cleanup and dispersal inevitably followed. We would listen to dire threats of what would happen if we lugged home anymore junk.

The thump of baseball in pood and the smack in glove from our yard seemed to send an extrasensory message to all the baseball-minded kids in Hannaford. Ole Thorseth was usually the first to arrive. Ole was three years older than I and a head taller than any of us. He could outthrow and outhit any kid in town. Singly and in groups the others trooped in. Most responded to nicknames—Fat, Sam, Curly, Baaba, Gaga, Claudie, Bud, Abutts, Wienie, and

Peasoup were pretty much the regulars. Some of these would be "stuck" with tagalong younger brothers who could always be used for fill-ins if we were short.

As soon as we could muster seven or eight players we would adjourn to our vacant lot baseball field. We usually started with a game of work-up, as this required only two batters at one time. The rest could be in the field. Someone would sing out, "First batter for a game of work-up!"

"Second batter!"

"Catcher!"

"Pitcher!"

"First base!"

And so it went, as far as there were players on hand. As a batter was put out, we would all move up a notch. Sooner or later Obie and Ole would become the batters together. Then began the nigh impossible task of getting one or both out. If this situation lasted too long, the game might even break up.

If and when a few more players arrived, someone would suggest choosing up sides. Usually, it was either "pitchers choose," or "catchers choose." If pitchers, it meant Ole and me—if catchers, Obie and Fat Johnson. Bumpy, being one of the youngest and smallest, was a second-string catcher. The process of choosing up sides was a deadly serious and ticklish business. Getting first choice was especially important. Players were chosen in order of their known ability. The tail-end choices were often the youngest and the tagalongs and were often regarded as liabilities—being almost sure "outs" upon their turns at bat. If there happened to be an uneven number of players, each chooser might generously waive his right to the extra man. The poorest player was always stuck out in right field where it was assumed he might do the least damage. Not too many balls were hit to right field.

Often Peasoup was the last player up for draft. "Since I got both Obie and Baaba you can have Peasoup for an extra player."

This magnanimous gesture on Ole's part might have once found favor. Now it was vehemently rejected. "Naw! He's yours! We don't want him!"

If Peasoup's feelings were hurt, he didn't show it. Whatever the disposition of his case, he knew that he would play right field and be at the bottom of the batting order. Sometimes our maneuvering would backfire. Another rookie, in a class with Peasoup, might show up, and he was automatically our property. There was tacit understanding that everyone got to play. Unhappy younger brothers reporting home could conceivably jeopardize your own appearance at the next game.

First choice was determined by the toss of a bat. As the bat was tossed by one of the choosers, the other, about to catch it, would holler out "full hand or none" or "one finger takes all!" Hands of the choosers moved alternately up the handle of the bat. Depending upon what had been called, either the last "full hand" or the last "one finger" on the bat handle earned first choice. Frequently the apparent loser's voice rose in protest, "C'mon, move y'er hand down where it b'longs—y'er cheatin'!"

Sometimes the ensuing argument could only be settled by "A'right, le's toss over."

We all knew for sure that Obie and Ole had some kind of trick or system. One or the other of the two invariably wound up with either "full hand" or "one finger" and first choice. Just as certainly they would each choose the other. Only our love for the game permitted us to be bamboozled this way time after time. After that fateful first choice that always put Obie and Ole together, the rest of the choosing was quite inconsequential. The outcome of the game was already determined. As a pitcher Ole was invincible, and the two together meant a one-two batting punch that we couldn't equal. Our only chance of getting them out at all depended upon whether they had their share of "tail-enders." Their earlier generosity in giving us a full team to their four players (catcher, pitcher, first baseman, and one fielder) had been exposed for the shabby trick it was.

Some kind of blowoff was inevitable. After all, there is a limit to what even a boy's spirit can take. It happened one day as my team was floundering on the short end of a 21 to 2 score. A momentary lapse on Ole's part had given us the two runs and averted the ignominy of another shutout. I had reached first base on an error, then Delbert closed his eyes and swung desperately at one of Ole's outcurves. The heavy bat, a cracked, taped-up discard of Hannaford's town team, met Ole's pitch squarely. The smack of bat against ball was sweet music in our ears. This time the ball sailed deep into right field and lit in the vicinity of Johnny Haugen's manure pile. By the time Peasoup had found the ball, both Del and I had crossed home plate.

Ole's scowl was clear warning that such a lucky accident wouldn't happen again in a year of Sundays.

Earlier in the game Ole had laid down a beautiful bunt along the third base line. Charging from the pitcher's box I managed to grab the ball and in the same motion uncork an accurate underhand throw to first baseman Wienie Alm. It was a close play. Ole claimed he was safe. My teammates howled, "Out!"

For once, Obie sided with us, "You were out alright, Ole— they gotcha by an eyelash."

"That was a perfect bunt," Ole protested, "He couldn't have got me!"

With pride in his voice Obie detailed my perfect fielding of the bunt. I in turn was proud of Obie for crediting me with a good play. Ole fumed for awhile before he finally conceded with considerably bad grace.

Thus this game had proceeded with more than the usual amount of bickering. We were up to bat for what we knew was our last time in the game. Ole had struck out our first two batters. I had stationed myself on the third base side of the diamond, well aware that that point was the closest in direct line to our yard. Whether by accident or design, my favorite slingshot and a few select pebbles were in a back pocket of my overalls. The opportune moment came. Ole bent over to inspect the pitcher's box. His posterior was toward me and offered an irresistible target. With the fastest draw in Hannaford, I aimed and fired.

Even before Ole's agonized yowl rent the air, I was off and running—in full flight toward the sanctuary of our yard. Ole's long strides quickly narrowed the gap between us and the sound of his pounding steps put terror in my heart. I could almost feel his outstretched, clutching hands on the nape of my scrawny neck as we rounded the nearest corner of our house.

Fortunately for me, Father was in the yard tinkering with our car. I darted behind the car and Ole pulled up short. He was still bawling and could scarcely get the accusatory words out, "He . . . he . . . he . . . Harvey . . . he hit me with a slingshot!"

Whether for emphasis or because of actual pain, Ole now had both hands massaging the injured part of his anatomy. The incriminating weapon was still clutched in my hand and I instinctively knew that it was useless to protest my innocence. Though from my point of view the provocation had been great, my abrupt action would scarcely find favor in Father's eyes.

"Give me your slingshot." Father's voice and eyes were stern. The evidence was in. I had been judged, and Father was ready to mete out the punishment. His powerful hands broke my beautiful slingshot into several pieces. The thought flashed through my mind, "I'll never find another tree 'crutch' as perfect as that one."

"Now get inside!" Father propelled me in the direction of the kitchen door with one hand and a resounding whap on my rear with the other, adding impetus to my departure.

I was not at all certain that Ole was satisfied with Father's dispensation of justice. Knowing Ole pretty well, I feared that the blow to his dignity on the diamond, even more than the hurt to his rear, would require personal vengeance. I carefully avoided any chance meeting with Ole for several days. Eventually the healing power of time soothed both Ole's ruffled feelings and his bruised behind.

Rivalry on the baseball field was resumed. Ole and Obie still managed to get on the same side. They continued to beat us with lopsided scores, but Ole may have been a little more cautious which way he positioned himself on the mound.

We did join forces for our games against the Walum "Wildcats." Walum was a neighboring town only three miles away. They had challenged us Bald Hill "Rats" with considerable bravado, and we had the honor and reputation of Hannaford to uphold. I don't recall that the Wildcats ever bested us in what became an annual home and home series—at least as long as Ole was our pitcher.

Our trip to Walum for a baseball game was an adventure in itself. Our team would walk the three miles along the right-of-way of the Northern Pacific branch line railroad track. Our pace was leisurely, and there were always diversions. Often we were strung out over a hundred yards, seeing who could walk the farthest balancing on a rail. Gophers abounded and offered elusive targets for our slingshots. It wasn't often that we hit one, but a well- placed pebble would make them dive down a hole with flick of tail. Our marksmanship often fared better on the glass insulators of the railroad telegraph poles. A heavier pebble and a square hit might cause a delightful explosion of shattering glass. I suspect that the railroad management might have taken a negative view of our traveling baseball team.

Little fanfare marked our team's arrival in Walum. The Wildcat's lookout, from atop a sidetracked box car, would spot us coming a good mile out and pass the word. The Wildcats would be warming up on their cow pasture playing field as we straggled in. As home team, they provided the baseball and an umpire. Often neither was too satisfactory. The umpire was usually one of their littlest kids, a substitute on their team. Once they even stuck us with a girl. If their baseball had too many fuzzy or broken stitches, we might condescend to offer ours.

Spectators were few and far between. A sprinkling of little kids and handful of silly, giggling girls usually watched us perform. The girls would stand or sit with their heads together and chatter unceasingly. Ole's manner on the pitching mound seemed a little more pompous than usual whenever girls were around.

The trip back to Hannaford after a game always lacked the gaiety of the outset. The thrill of victory, with its accompaniment of braggadocio over individual exploits, sustained us for perhaps the first mile of the homeward journey. Thereafter, spirits and tails alike started to droop. Each mile seemed like two. Tireless irrepressible Bumpy would invariably be in the vanguard. Just as surely, Del and Baaba would be at the tail end of the stragglers.

The thought of the supper that Mother would have waiting is all that sustained us on the arduous, homeward trek. Of such stuff were Hannaford's heroes, the Bald Hill Rats, made.

3

Bumpy, First in Their Hearts

IT was inevitable that Bumpy should find favor with all who came to know him, and that included almost everyone in Hannaford. His sunny disposition, unflagging energy, and oft-exhibited pluck endeared him to the hearts of grown-ups.

If Bumpy turned up missing at mealtime, Mother didn't worry too much. She knew he was having dinner or supper somewhere. Since we had no telephone, she was not often informed. Bumpy would ingratiate himself with older ladies who had no one to run their errands. He knew who baked the best cookies and whose apples were the sweetest. I think Mother understood that Bumpy's presence brought a touch of happiness to many a lonely home.

Running errands was only a sideline with Bumpy. He preferred more manly pursuits. He might ride all morning with Frank Olson, Hannaford's drayman, on his appointed rounds. Frank drove a team of horses, and people grew accustomed to seeing a familiar diminutive figure alongside of Frank on the high spring seat. Frank would meet the trains, and while he would handle cream cans and boxes of freight, Bumpy would hold the reins of the placid team. It made a boy look mighty important up there, and Bumpy relished his role. Though the stolid horses, accustomed to clattering cans and train whistle alike, stood with drooping heads, Bumpy admonished them constantly: "Whoa, boy, whoa! easy there, steady boy, whoa!" After a forenoon's work, such a valued helper had earned his dinner at Frank's table.

Walter Larson operated the town's livery stable. Bumpy found this a busy, exciting place to be when not on the dray. While self-appointed, he soon considered himself Walt's indispensable right-hand man. He could lead horses to the watering trough out back and poke down hay from the loft. When there was barn cleaning to be done, Bumpy pitched manure with enthusiasm. On one such occasion, working with his usual reckless abandon, a misdirected forkful overshot the spreader wagon and splashed over Walt on the other side. Walt later confessed to Father that for a moment a beautiful friendship was in jeopardy.

Father would either borrow or rent a horse from Walt to use in plowing our garden and in planting potatoes. Later in the summer we would use the horse in cultivating. As Father struggled with the hand-held plow or cultivator, Bumpy liked to sit astride the animal and guide it up the furrows. He also felt it his obligation to ride the horse on the return trip to Walt's livery stable. Doubtless Walt sensed a growing attachment between Bumpy and the swaybacked old mare. One day Bumpy came home leading the now unharnessed nag by its halter rope. He was jumping with joy as he babbled, "Papa! Papa! Look! Walt gave Nell to me. Can we keep her, Papa? Can we keep her? Huh?"

Father struggled with this for a moment. I know the harshness in his voice was evoked by anger over Walt Larson's thoughtless prank. "You know, Son, that we have no place to keep a horse. Now you take Nell back to the livery barn, and you tell Walt—'no horse!' Do you understand? No HORSE!''

Walt apologized to Father later and confessed that his amusement over what was meant to be a joke at Father's expense turned quickly to consternation when a crestfallen Bumpy tearfully returned old Nell. Walt made amends by taking Bumpy to a circus at the county seat the following Saturday.

Next to his feeling for Father, Bumpy reserved his greatest loyalty and affection for Jack Wills. Jack was a grizzled, rugged Scotsman. One of the early pioneers in the county, he had retired from the farm in 1916 to live in Hannaford. Here he kept several milch cows and also busied himself in an extensive garden and orchard. One of his sons farmed the homeplace.

Mr. and Mrs. Wills regarded Bumpy as they might have a favorite grandson. When Mr. Wills was in town (he made almost daily trips to his nearby farm) Bumpy tagged his footsteps. They were generous footsteps to follow, since Mr. Wills stood about six feet four. Bumpy was always small for his age, and the two companions offered an odd contrast.

All during the summer months Bumpy was engaged to take Mr. Wills's cows to and from a community pasture along Bald Hill Creek. The cows, led by old Bluebell, knew the way and Bumpy's main task was to follow along and open and close the pasture gate. The Willses lived in the same part of town as we did, and we were reminded of Bumpy's coming and going by the jangle of the bell that was strapped to Bluebell's neck. The cows always walked in single file, with Bluebell setting the pace. Bringing up the rear, his bare feet padding along the dusty, littered path, would be Bumpy. His short strides necessitated sporadic trotting in order to keep up.

Bumpy usually went to fetch the cows in late afternoon. Often he would find them waiting at the pasture gate. Occasionally they delayed their coming and Bumpy might have to walk way up the pasture searching, listening for Bluebell's tinkling bell to disclose their whereabouts.

A sudden summer thunderstorm caught Bumpy once in the pasture's farthest reach. When hailstones began to pelt his bare head, a frightened Bumpy sought shelter in a small clump of straggly trees. The good Lord was looking after the little cowherd that day. Bumpy spotted the rusted metal bowl from a cream separator atop a pile of discarded junk. Held over his head and shoulders, it provided a shield against the driving hail. The din of the hailstones pounding on that inverted bowl left Bumpy's ears ringing for days afterward.

While the episode was a truly frightening one for everyone concerned, it did clothe Bumpy with a hero's mantle. Everyone was thankful, of course, that Bumpy had escaped injury and had high praise for his presence of mind. Bumpy accepted the accolades with an "oh that was nuthin' " mien, but he made the most of his fleeting fame.

Accustomed as we all were to Bumpy's sunny disposition and the exuberant gusto he brought to bear on every challenge, his sudden rebellion one summer day left us all bewildered. The day had started well with all the promise of another blissful interlude in a so-far uneventful summer. Bumpy, Del, and I had been dutifully enrolled in a vacation Bible school. There had been only the usual amount of grumbling; compliance was taken for granted. To impatient lads, even a week's curtailment of regular pursuits seemed an infringement of some magnitude.

It was as we were preparing to return for the afternoon session that Bumpy announced his disinclination to go back—that day or any other day. Mother stared in disbelief. From Del it might not have been as startling—but Bumpy!

Wheedling made no dent in Bumpy's defiance. We were standing in the yard, Bumpy maintaining a discreet distance, with a wary eye on all of us. If Mother advanced a step, Bumpy retreated a step. Mother was growing desperate. Afternoon classes would soon be starting. To break the impasse, Mother sent Obie indoors to summon Father.

Father sized up the situation in a glance. "Come here, Bumpy." It was the voice and manner Father used for command. Undaunted, Bumpy stood his ground. As Father moved resolutely toward him, Bumpy turned and took off running. He headed up the road with Father in plodding pursuit. A safe distance ahead Bumpy would slow to a walk. Then, as Father's longer steps narrowed the gap, Bumpy would again break into a run. To the edge of town and beyond it the relentless chase continued.

The road they were on paralleled the railroad track, though there was some distance between. About a mile out of town the main road disappeared over the brow of a hill and a side road led in the direction of the railroad tracks. As soon as Bumpy knew that he was out of Father's sight beyond the hill, he doubled back toward town along the railroad track.

Father plodded wearily up and over the hill, unaware that his quarry had given him the slip. Even before Father gave up and started to retrace his steps, Bumpy was home.

Now it was Obie's turn to take up the chase. This time Bumpy headed out in a different direction. Across Mother's garden and through neighbors' yards, Bumpy led Obie a merry chase. There was no letting up now, and Obie was right on Bumpy's tail when they hit a freshly plowed field. The soft footing gave Bumpy a temporary advantage. His lighter weight and bare feet fared better here than did Obie in heavy shoes. Circling and dodging, Bumpy managed to elude Obie's grasp, until he slipped and fell exhausted. Too tired to struggle further, he was led docilely by the hand back to face his waiting father.

The chase on the hot, dusty road apparently had taken its toll of Father. Neither spanking nor lecture was forthcoming. He listened with quiet compassion to the tearful account of a little boy's dislike for vacation school. Then with tender hands touching the dust-stained cheeks of his errant son, we were amazed to hear Father pronounce, "All right, son, you won't have to go back—no more Bible school for now." He followed his dispensation of mercy with a brusque admonition, "From now on, son, you obey your mother! You hear?"

Father's edict was not meant to include Del and me. We continued the daily round of vacation Bible school. To declare that we harbored no resentment might appear as a noble gesture, but would certainly ill reflect what we were taught in Bible school. It wasn't that we didn't love Bumpy. As kid brothers go, he was certainly one of the best. Bumpy, on the other hand, idolized his brothers. Perhaps it was inevitable that we used him.

If he tagged along when we went trapping or hunting, we generously let him carry the game. After we acquired a .22-calibre rifle, we often would bag a jackrabbit or two. Bumpy might lug a "jack" that was almost as long as he was tall for miles without complaining.

We would also post Bumpy as our lookout when we raided Mr. Wigen's garden. Mr. Wigen was a neighbor whose carrots and peas always tasted better than our own. And he had a strawberry patch. His garden was separated from his house and yard by several rows of trees. A shed that he used for storing his car and garden tools stood in these trees midway between house and garden. We would boost Bumpy to the roof of this shed, where he would keep an eye out for Mr. Wigen. For his sacrifice and risk taking, we would generously share a bit of the loot.

Del and I also kept a covetous eye on Mr. Wills's apple orchard. This was surrounded by a rather high and difficult-to- climb fence. Also the apple trees were under ready surveillance from the windows of the Wills house. Since Bumpy stood high in the Wills's favor and had free movement within their yard, Del and I tried time and time again to inveigle Bumpy into tossing apples over the fence. Here, however, Bumpy drew the line. His loyalty to Mr. Wills outweighed his trust of his brothers.

There were times when Del and I preferred not to have Bumpy's company. He was hard to shake, however, and sometimes we resorted to desperate measures. We would truss him lightly with a length of clothesline rope and then take off on the run. By the time he freed himself, Del and I would be out of sight.

It was Bumpy's prowess on the Hannaford ski jump that really put his brothers to shame.

Bald Hill Creek afforded year-round pleasure and challenge to the boys growing up in Hannaford. The frozen creek itself provided miles of adventuresome ice skating. Mink abounded along its banks and were sought by eager young trappers. The gently sloping hills were ideal for skiing, sledding, and tobogganing.

Ski jumping came into its own in Hannaford with the arrival of Norwegian-born Peter Falstad. Pete had begun his skiing in his native Norway. Arriving in the United States as a young man, Pete soon took his place among some of the best-known skiers in this country. Along with Alf Engen, Torger Tokle, and Casper Oimon, Pete achieved fame as a ski jumper. He was a member of the United States Olympic skiing team in 1924.

While the hills along the Bald Hill must have appeared rather insignificant to this renowned ski jumper, he, nonetheless, was not to be denied participation in the sport he had grown up with. In short order Pete had designed and constructed a ski slide. This consisted of a steeply sloping surface suspended from a tall steel tower. This ski slide was perched at the brow of the steepest slope overlooking Bald Hill Creek. The natural valley slope had been carved (through excavation) into an even steeper landing surface beneath the jump.

The jumper, with skis carried on his shoulder, had to laboriously climb a set of narrow steps to the top of the slide. A single handrail along the outer edge of the steep slide provided precarious support to the climber. Once at the top he stepped onto his skis and adjusted the bindings. An experienced jumper would launch his body sharply over the edge in order to attain the utmost speed down the long and precipitous takeoff. To maintain his balance on this abrupt drop he would have to lean forward in a deep crouch. The takeoff leveled off for a few feet before ending suddenly high above the ground. As the end of the jump rushed forward to meet him, the skier would straighten his body and lift his arms to increase the distance of his jump.

Pete's jumps were something to behold! His lean, lithe figure hurtled down the slide and out into space. His control or style in the air and his landing were judged to be well-nigh perfect. Frequently he would almost overjump the limited landing, thus endangering both his life and limb. It was little wonder that people came from long distances to watch this great skier perform. Hannaford residents were mighty proud of Pete and the Olympic team emblem emblazoned on his trim blue sweater and stocking cap.

During the mid-1920s, several jumping tournaments were held in Hannaford each winter and would ordinarily attract other well-known and capable skiers. Casper Oimon made frequent appearances. Hannaford, too, had other hardy local ski enthusiasts who tried mightily to emulate Pete's jumping feats. Marcus Hakken was perhaps the oldest of the regular contestants and always provided the comic relief in a tourney. His portly figure coming off the jump bore a slight resemblance to an airborne elephant. His stocky arms flailed like the blades of twin windmills as he fought for

Peter Falsted, from Norway, came to Hannaford, designed and built our first ski slide for ski jumping.

Bumpy astride Old Nell from Walt's livery stable.

A rig such as rented from Walt's.

distance and balance. Otto Polson—next to Ole Thorseth, Obie's best pal—was without question the most adept of the younger skiers.

Leave it to Bumpy to wiggle his way into this select group of performers. Bumpy, like the rest of us, learned to ski on Bald Hill Creek. We practiced on small jumps built by shoveling up a mound of snow a few feet high. In short order Bumpy graduated. He had secretly tried out the ski slide and discovered that he could negotiate it and wind up in one piece. I think poor Father almost swallowed his snuff when Bumpy announced that he was going to jump in an upcoming tournament. He had already signed up in the junior division.

When Father realized that Bumpy had been risking his neck on the slide by jumping without bindings on his skis, he had our local harnessmaker make some.

On the day of the tournament, Father, Mother, Obie, Del, and I joined the throng of spectators below the ski slide to watch Bumpy make his debut. The huge number 12 fastened across Bumpy's chest and back hung like an apron almost to his knees. We watched apprehensively as the tiny figure made its way to the top of the slide. His head was barely visible over the top edge when he was announced.

An instant later Bumpy was on his way down. He squatted so low, it appeared that he was sitting on his skis. He went over the jump in the same crouched position and barely cleared the top of the landing. He probably sailed thirty feet through the air and hit the landing with skis wide spread. Momentarily he teetered precariously, and the crowd anticipated a spill. Miraculously he recovered his balance and scooted on down almost to the creek bed itself before coming to a stop. The crowd gave him a tremendous hand, and I must admit that we were all pretty proud of our Bumpy.

He made two more successful jumps that day, and although he did not place in the junior division, he did win the hearts of everyone watching. In ensuing tournaments, Bumpy continued to be the darling of the crowds who came to watch. Though Bumpy received this adulation modestly enough, it was again that "oh, that was nuthin' " air that bothered Del and me. Obie accepted Bumpy's triumphs with considerably more grace.

Finally Del and I could no longer stand the ignominy of being outdone by our kid brother. Early one Saturday morning we took our skis, eluded both Bumpy and Obie, and covertly made our way to the ski slide. We knew that it had been readied for an upcoming tournament and would be in tiptop shape.

We determinedly made our way to the top of the slide and strapped on our skis. We were both perfectly willing to let the other go first. I would resolutely move to the edge and peer over. Cowed by the sight of that dizzying descent, I would back off and Del would take my place. Then it was his turn to "chicken out." This procrastination continued indeterminably until we were both shivering, partly from cold and partly, I suppose, from fright.

Del had yielded the starting position to me for the umpteenth time. Again I stood poised at the edge with only a halfhearted resolve to make the attempt. I must have inadvertently moved too close to the brink. I'm certain that I did not shove off by my own free will. I later accused Del of giving me a little nudge, but he vehemently denied this.

At any rate, I suddenly found myself plunging downward. Completely out of balance, I fell backward on my skis. Soon I was slithering and sliding sideways down the takeoff. Fortunately, the ends of my skis did not catch on the guard railing supports. My unscheduled journey down the face of the slide ended abruptly when I slid off the end of the jump and plopped unceremoniously into the flax straw below. The straw cushioned my fall, and after a moment of initial shock I knew that nothing was hurt except my dignity.

From the top of the slide a frantic Del hollered, "Harvey! Harvey! Are you all right?" I had disappeared from his sight after my drop. I struggled to untangle myself and unbuckle my ski bindings. Then still spitting flax straw and dust, I staggered out to where Del could see that I was still in one piece. Without further ado, Del unfastened his ski bindings and made his way afoot down the steps—carrying his skis. Clearly Del had decided that discretion was now the better part of valor.

We told no one about our fiasco until years later. At the time it would have been humiliation simply unbearable.

Our grudging admiration for Bumpy's indomitable spirit was growing. He was fast becoming a legend in Hannaford. Boyhood years passed all too quickly on the Bald Hill.

4

Train Whistle in the Night

THE lonely whistle of a steam locomotive making its throbbing way across the prairie in the dead of night was enough to set a boy to dreaming. Where had it come from? Whither bound? All too soon, the romantic night song of the trains faded into the hoarse rumble of the workaday world.

Even so, we found it exciting to go to the depot at traintime. Where the shimmering rails disappeared on the horizon, a smudge of black smoke would signal an oncoming steam locomotive long before we heard its faint, far-off whistle. Gradually the tiny speck in the distance took shape and became an onrushing giant. The hum of wheels on rails suddenly became a roaring clatter as the train moved across the long wooden trestle that spanned Ball Hill Creek. Bell clanging, the long passenger train moved majestically into the Hannaford station.

The engineer usually rewarded our presence with a cheery wave as he brought the hissing, clanking monster to a jarring halt right before our wondering eyes. From the steps of a coach, the brakeman would swing easily to the platform and place an extra mounting step for passengers.

For the next several minutes the depot platform was the scene of feverish activity. There were happy greetings and earnest good-byes. Drummers went their solitary way, easily distinguishable by bowler, cigar, and sample cases. The depot agent trundled his wooden-wheeled express wagon, piled high with suitcase, trunk, and cream can, alongside the baggage car. Sacks of mail were loaded and unloaded. The gauntleted engineer in gray striped coveralls and cap, with oil can in hand, hovered tenderly around his panting engine.

The conductor, resplendent in gold-buttoned blue serge, maintained a circumspect watch. He was truly monarch of all he surveyed, and he played his role to the hilt. The grandiose flourish with which he consulted his magnificent gold watch was a gesture befitting a superb actor or king. At the precise second, he sounded his stentorian " 'Board—all aboard." This was accompanied a moment later by an arm signal to his waiting engineer.

With a final warning toot of whistle and amid a cloud of steam, the high wheeler started the train moving with a scarcely perceptible jerk. As the cars slid by, strangers would peer out at us from the windows. We might see the broadly grinning face of a friendly porter. Sometimes we would glimpse elegant diners being served by immaculate white-coated waiters. The conductor, master performer to the end, stood unperturbed as the cars gained momentum. When it looked almost certain that he would be left behind, he would grab the fast-moving handrail of the last coach and swing nimbly aboard. From his vantage point on the rear observation deck he would favor us with a final benignant wave. Then he turned and disappeared inside his retreating domain.

The depot platform was suddenly a forlorn and empty place. Bulging sacks of mail were on their way to the post office, piled high in the box of George's tin lizzie. Frank's dray, loaded with incoming boxes and barrels, was usually the last vehicle to depart. Only a little boy lingered, seated now on the edge of the rough, planked platform with bare feet swinging in rhythm to the fading clickety-clack from the shimmering rails. As he gazed at the dwindling smudge of black smoke, he knew that one day he would be aboard that departing train. Only the role was unclear—engineer, brakeman, mail clerk, conductor, or one of the elegant diners? With such transient visions dancing in his head, bare feet skipped gaily down the dusty path toward home.

The morning westbound train coming in from Minneapolis, on the Great Northern line, was also the carrier of exciting packages from mail-order houses in the cities. We knew almost to the day when merchandise ordered from the big "wish books" would arrive. There was no dearth of volunteers to run uptown to the post office once the morning train whistled its approach. Cautious Del would note the color and density of the locomotive's smoke before volunteering his services. Only a plume of black smoke draped back over the approaching coaches would impel Del to make the trip. The fates had proved Del inerrant in reading the smoke signals. Black meant "package on board" to clairvoyant Del.

Our stringent family budget did not permit indiscriminate choosing and ordering. The need for an item had to be real. Shoes tattered beyond repair or overalls that would simply hold no more patches were legitimate. A dollar ninety-eight cent baseball glove might be in the picture if it were a birthday, or if the recipient had earned and painfully saved his pennies. The concept of opportunity cost, though not identified by name, was an ever-present reality to us. Whenever a choice was made, something else was sacrificed. Because of this, particular mail-order purchases are etched in my mind: the dashing navy blue-with-white trim, one-piece cotton bathing suit; the sixteen-inch, oil-tanned welted boots (destined for a scorched, fiery demise on a foolhardy ice-skating escapade); my first long pants; the full-sized Tris Speaker fielder's glove with molded pocket; the one-piece BVD underwear; a genuine badger-bristle shaving brush and a Gem safety razor. Each in turn marked a red-letter day in my life.

The railroad tracks and yard held a well-nigh irresistible fascination for adventuresome Hannaford lads. Sometimes our walk along the tracks was prompted by Mother's need for fuel for her cookstove. Hannaford was a coaling station for the steam locomotives. The locomotive would usually be uncoupled from its train of cars before puffing up to the coal dock or chute. The fireman would clamber from cab to tender and swing the loading chute into position. Chunks of coal tumbled by gravity until the tender was heaped to overflowing. Lumps of this coal might later be dislodged from precarious perch atop the load and scattered along the right-of-way. Often we could scavenge a pailful in a half-mile walk.

Burning this reclaimed coal on a steady basis produced a heavy accumulation of soot in the stovepipe and chimney. This in turn exposed us to the danger of frequent chimney fires. At times the section of stovepipe leading to the chimney would glow cherry red from the intense heat of the burning soot. I am certain that at such times Mother was alarmed, but she rose to the occasion and seemingly subdued the raging inferno by propelling a few tablespoons of salt into the pipe through the damper opening. Outside, soot and sparks rained down on the wooden shingles. The good Lord was with us, because we never had to spread a fire alarm. When a building in Hannaford did catch on fire it usually burned to the ground. The town had a fire hall with a rope-pulled alarm bell mounted overhead. Its raucous clang at least summoned people to watch the conflagration. Hannaford boasted no city water, and the hand-drawn pumper could only operate in close proximity to a well.

A walk along the tracks yielded windfalls other than coal. We always kept our eyes open for signs of a hotbox mishap. A journal box on a heavily loaded freight car would sometimes overheat by friction. Telltale smoke, or at night a red glow, would signal the trouble to a watchful brakeman on the observation seat of the caboose. He in turn would relay a trouble signal to the engineer. The train would be stopped and a brakeman would make his way to the crippled car. The babbitt metal bearings in the journal box were made of an antifriction alloy and packed in an oil-impregnated cotton waste for lubrication. To correct a hotbox, the smouldering waste and molten babbitt had to be removed and the bearings replaced. The molten babbit would congeal in grotesque shapes as it spattered on the gravel roadbed. We would retrieve these splashes of metal for remelting and casting in crude sand molds.

Obie's backyard foundry consisted of a rock-lined firepit and a discarded iron skillet. The babbitt had a fairly low melting point and could be separated from the small rocks and charred waste. Not all of the items that Obie poured were recognizable or of much use. There were exceptions. Crudely formed animals, toy soldiers, and medallions had barter value among the unsophisticated younger set.

Obie's crowning achievement was a usable and much admired shot put. A hollow rubber ball buried in sand served as a spherical mold. The molten metal was funneled in through an exposed opening. With some buffing, the resulting metal ball was reasonably round, was perhaps three and one-half inches in diameter, and weighed a bit over eight pounds. It served admirably, and some mighty heaves resulted. Father accepted the resulting divots in an already battered lawn as part of the price of raising boys.

An added bonus from the hotbox scene was often a fusee—a kind of flare used as a warning signal and trouble light by the trainmen. The fusee had a spiked base so that it could be set firmly on the wooden tie. Generally the discarded fusee had burned for half or more of its twelve-inch length, but occasionally a whole one was retrieved. The unlit fusee was apparently thrown aside if it failed to burn when the igniting cap was struck. The fortunate finder waved the trophy triumphantly and was much envied. We were usually able to relight these flares with a generous application of matches.

An intriguing part of the railroad yards was the stockyard. Every midwestern rail stop had one. Cattle, sheep, and hogs were brought here to be loaded into stock cars for the haul to distant markets. The stockyard was constructed of sturdy wooden planking. Its many holding pens, with huge swinging gates and loading chute, challenged young Tarzans to climb, swing, and explore. At times its upper reaches might be the battlements of a castle or the crow's nest of a fast-sailing clipper.

Loading days might find us clambering to a top railing to watch the bawling, stubborn animals being urged up the ramp and into the waiting stock car. Punctilious timing of the loading assured that the loaded cars were ready for pickup as scheduled. A stock train would become progressively longer as consignments were added at successive shipping points along the line. Representatives of the owners would accompany the livestock to market. A single passenger coach near the rear of the train was their conveyance. Bumpy's friend, Mr. Wills, often made the trip for the Hannaford shippers. I know that Bumpy anticipated the day when he might accompany Mr. Wills.

Only when the last fractious steer had been prodded and tail-twisted up the ramp and the sliding door clanged shut would the enthralled spectators remember unfinished errands or waiting dinners.

Just as the stockyard provided overnight shelter, feed, and water for the animals, it was also a haven for the hobos who rode the freight trains. They might sleep under the roof in the hay-filled manger or cook their mulligan near the pump out behind. Exploring lads cautiously gave the stockyard jungle a wide berth if they suspected tramps were around. There was almost daily evidence of the hobos' activities throughout the lazy days of summer. Battered, blackened cooking pots and cans were apparently rinsed after use and considerately stacked for brethren who followed. We respected their communal possessions and were shocked and frightened when some person or persons shot these pitiful utensils full of holes. For a time we were fearful of retaliation by the tramps.

We often saw them walk past our place on their way up town. Invariably a bedroll or packsack was slung across their backs. Infrequently, one would stop and ask Mother for a bite to eat. Apparently these "knights of the road" noted and respected our modest circumstances. More prosperous-looking homes were the ones usually targeted. Mother knew that the tramps helped themselves to some of our sweet corn and potatoes. This had her blessing. She remarked that these poor, homeless men were somebody's sons and that they got hungry just as we did. As the nights grew frosty in late September the hobos no longer stopped off at Hannaford. Like the migratory birds, they sojourned in warmer climes.

Yet another attraction in the railroad yards was an unused grain elevator. It was intended to be off limits for trespassers, but the curiosity of boys was not to be denied. We discovered a way to get inside and explored it from top to bottom. Some of its lower reaches were infested with rats. Musty, spongy piles of dusty screenings were honeycombed with their runways. The scurrying rats made elusive targets for our ever-present slingshots. Expert marksmen as we were on stationary targets, we did little to reduce the rat population.

A hand-powered lift cage gave access clear to the cupola of the elevator. Two or three of us could stand on the small wooden platform and counterbalance the movable weights. Even slight hand-over-hand pressure on the center rope would propel us up or down. If danger were involved, we were ignorant of or ignored it. Mothers would, I'm sure, have taken a dim view of many of our capers. Knowing how mothers tend to get upset over so many things, "mum" was the word. A violation of this code was not taken lightly, and life could become quite miserable for the tattler. The favorite recrimination was the repetitious group chant:

> Tattletale, tattletale, hanging on the bull's tail;
> When the bull began to walk, tattletale began to talk!

Pigeons often strutted around the cupola roof. We would stand on the ground below and fire pebbles at them with our slingshots. At that distance, the trajectory of our missiles became a broadly looping curve and the almost-spent stones pattered harmlessly on the shingled roof. The pigeons were quite disdainful of our efforts, and even a lucky direct hit would elicit only a brief flurry. Of the dozen or so pigeons that frequented the elevator roof, one stood out. He was a trifle larger than the others and seemed to be the leader of the flock. Somebody named him "Old Blue" and the moniker stuck. If a well-placed pebble alarmed Old Blue into precipitous flight, the rest of the pigeons followed. It was inevitable that he became our primary target.

The flock often shuttled between the elevator roof and the top of the coal chute. I suspected that they nested in the upper part of the chute, since they often disappeared into its upper reaches. There appeared to be an aperture of some kind through which they entered.

The futile pursuit of Old Blue extended well into a second summer. I think every boy in our neighborhood aspired to be the conqueror of this elusive quarry. I knew that it would take a more deadly weapon than my trusty slingshot to fell Old Blue.

Then fate seemingly took a hand. I spotted this exciting ad in the spring: "Sell only 72 packages of garden seeds to earn this handsome .22-calibre rifle." It took a lot of tearful pleading to win Father's consent to order the seeds. When he grudgingly yielded, it was probably with the thought that I would never sell all seventy-two packs and would settle for a lesser and, in his eyes, more acceptable prize. Father underestimated my determination. Day after day—from door to door—my sales pitch was the same: "Do you want to buy some garden seeds? They're only a dime." Not too original, and not too effective. At times I despaired and almost gave up. It appeared that I had glutted the Hannaford market. No one wanted the last fourteen packages. I believe Mother was sorely tempted to help me out and take them off my hands, but Father was adamant. If I didn't sell them, they could be returned to the seed company. Then came the windfall. A lady whose home I had purposely bypassed stopped me on the street one day. "Young man, are you the one selling garden seeds?"

"Yes, M-m-m-mam," I stammered.

She looked over my remaining stock and selected eight packages. Then she steered me to my final customer. The six remaining packages were sold.

Father was unbelieving until I counted out my money, seven dollars and twenty cents. I don't think he shared my elation, but he shrugged and accepted the inevitable.

Each day for the next two weeks I ran to the post office. To an impatient boy it was a trying time—a seemingly endless wait. Finally the package came. I ran every step of the way home, my heart pounding with excitement and boundless joy.

Obie and Del were on hand for the unwrapping. The little rifle wasn't too prepossessing—at least in Obie's eyes. "Some rifle—huh! It looks like a toy." Its overall length was only twenty-four inches. It was a single-shot Hamilton, made to fire .22 shorts. The brass barrel was encased in a wraparound sheath of pressed steel. The stock was almost ugly, being machine sawed from a flat piece of half-inch board. Obie's unkind assessment of my hard-earned gun did not leave me crestfallen for long. After all, it was a .22 rifle, and it did shoot real bullets.

The little weapon was quite inaccurate and perhaps unsafe as well. Occasionally I could hit a tin can from ten short paces away. I didn't get too much chance to practice my shooting as the cartridges were twenty-five cents for a box of fifty. A box had to last a long time. Father urged me to be very careful where I pointed the gun, and I was not to shoot at songbirds. Gophers, crows, and English sparrows were legitimate targets. Nothing was said about pigeons.

I could not get Old Blue out of my mind. I took a few potshots at him as he strutted on the ridgepole of the elevator cupola. Needless to say, I didn't touch a feather and decided to save my ammunition. The distance was too great.

Then came the big idea! Perhaps I could stalk Old Blue in his hideout high within the coal chute. My opportunity came on a Sunday afternoon. Obie and Del had gone swimming. Bumpy was on a berry-picking outing with the Willses. I managed to leave the house surreptitiously while Father was napping and Mother was occupied in her flower garden. The little Hamilton .22 was cradled in my arm.

I was quite familiar with the coal chute, since Father had once been employed there. His job had been to unload the cars of coal into the pits and to operate the huge gas engine that powered the endless belt lifts. One of my assigned tasks had been to bring him his lunch. Father's face and clothes would be black with coal dust. The whites of his eyes rolled upward as he gulped coffee from the tin pail. I wondered why Father had to work at such a dirty job. I often stayed and watched him at work. Sometimes I explored dusty cat-walks and stairs.

On this particular afternoon I had one purpose in mind—to find Old Blue. He wasn't on the roof of the elevator, so that made the coal chute a likely bet. I managed to boost myself up onto the first work ledge or platform. A dimly lit and narrow passageway led to an inner shaft where coal was elevated to the overhead loading bin. A built-on wall ladder reached skyward toward cable pulley wheels in the very top of the structure. Somewhere, far overhead in the shadows, I could hear the soft cooing of pigeons. I was hot on the trail of Old Blue.

Clutching the little .22 in one hand I started to climb. The steps of the seldom used ladder were slippery with an accumulated layer of coal dust. Carefully, one precarious handhold at a time, I edged upward. Dislodged particles of coal dust eddied about me and started my eyes to blinking. At times I paused in the upward climb to catch my breath and to free one arm to wipe my face.

Only once did I dare to look down. The abysmal blackness of the coal pits below brought a quaking, hollow feeling to the pit of my stomach. Weak and visibly trembling, I still pushed upward. There was more light near the top and finally I could make out the shadowy outlines of the pigeons. By now, they were aware of my intrusion and were uneasily moving about.

Up, up, up, I struggled! Suddenly I saw Old Blue. Poised for flight, he was moving uneasily along a window ledge with head cocked warily in my direction. His low, throaty coo clearly sounded an alert to his nervous companions.

The moment of reckoning had come. To secure myself, I wrapped one arm firmly around the closest crosspiece. With the free arm I extended the little .22, pistol fashion, in the direction of Old

Blue. It was impossible to aim the wavering weapon; all I could do was point it in the direction of his handsome, glistening breast. When he momentarily paused in his uneasy shuffle, I squeezed the trigger. With the sharp crack of the little gun, all hell broke loose. The startled pigeons fluttered madly around, dislodging cascades of coal dust and roosting debris on my head. In his death throes, Old Blue began a wildly gyrating descent. His madly flapping wings beat further torrents of coal dust from walls and cables.

The gun dropped from my unnerved hand as I clutched for further support and hung on for dear life. Far below I heard the thud of Old Blue's body as it struck the coal. Then it was quiet, and I became violently sick to my stomach. Alternately sobbing and vomiting, I clung to my dizzy perch.

Some minutes elapsed before I could steel myself to start down. It was a slow and tortuous process—one groping step at a time—down, down, down. Finally, after what seemed an eternity to a shocked and frightened boy, my feet touched the catwalk. I now stood only ten or twelve feet above the coal in the pit. When I saw the still body of Old Blue lying there on the coal I started to retch all over again. Those limp, outstretched wings would never beat the air again. I felt no elation—only sadness. There was no sign of the Hamilton .22. It must have bounced and slid into some inaccessible corner of the pit.

Mother took one startled look at her grimy, disheveled son and moved swiftly to the cleaning and scrubbing task. She put hot water in the washtub and handed me soap and towel. She laid out clean shirt and overalls and only then put her thoughts into words, "Where in the world have you been and what have you been up to?" Noting my pale, stricken face and hesitancy to answer, Mother did not delve any further. I think she knew where I'd been. She was no stranger to greasy coal dust. During his stint in the coal dock, Father had come home almost as dirty every day.

I told no one about the incident. When asked about the Hamilton .22, I tersely replied, "It's lost." Del noted one day that Old Blue was no longer with the pigeons. I don't think either Del or Obie would have believed my story had I told them. They had far more faith in their slingshots than in my Hamilton .22.

Diesel engines replaced the steam locomotives—no more black smudge of smoke on the horizon. Though the first passenger diesels went into operation in 1934 and the first freight diesels in 1941, the steam locomotive continued to rule as king of the rails in much of the country until after World War II. The last of the steam giants had quite a streamlined appearance. The coal chute and the stockyard are gone. Cattle are trucked to market. Passenger service on the Hannaford run was discontinued some years ago. The depot with its once bustling waiting room and ever-chattering telegraph has been removed. The shimmering rails remain, and mile-long freights rumble through. Barefoot boys no longer venture there, picking coal and searching for babbitt. At times, in the dead of night, I awaken and hear a far-off train whistle. For me, the sound is not the same, the dreams are far removed.

5

Kaiser Bill Went up the Hill

WE first heard about the Huns from Ole Thorseth. When Ole hinted darkly about the terrible deeds perpetrated by these cruel villains, we were shocked and terrified. We hadn't the faintest idea who these monsters were or where or why their atrocities were committed. We would not, however, give Ole the satisfaction of knowing that we were unaware of what these Huns were doing. Far better to let Ole ramble on than to display our ignorance and give him the chance to gloat as he usually did: "You mean you haven't heard that?" or, "You mean you don't know that?" Incredulous sarcasm was in the question. Ole could sure make us feel like dummies.

We were to learn that the dreaded Huns in this instance were German soldiers who had violated Belgium neutrality, whatever that meant. In their march through Belgium, it was said, they had cut off children's hands and bayoneted women and children.

Ole had an advantage over us in that the Thorseth household received a daily newspaper. News of events beyond the Hannaford city limits traveled slowly. A town crier of sorts was drayman, Frank Olson. Perhaps, because in the line of his work he met all the trains, he seemed the first to get news. Also, being a garrulous individual, he delighted in purveying what he heard to anyone willing to listen. Some folks, including Mother, regarded Frank as an old gossip. Often he was referred to as Hannaford's "Penny Press." Father took a more tolerant view. He felt that for better or for worse, Frank rendered the town a service.

Frank was more excited than usual on the May morning of 1915 when he spread the news that the *Lusitania* had been sunk by a German submarine off the Irish coast. The war in Europe still seemed remote and far removed, but there was a growing awareness of the peoples involved. Most of the residents of Hannaford were either of Scandinavian descent or of English, Scotch, or Irish origin. Only a sprinkling were of German background. It was not surprising, then, that they saw much of the war through English eyes. Grandfather Rasmussen had come to America to avoid military conscription in his native Denmark. He hoped that his adopted country would not become involved in the troubles of Europe. More than ever, the sinking of the *Lusitania* identified Germany as an enemy. I overheard Walt Larson opine to Father that the Hun would have to be stopped.

I suspect that both Father and Mother had inherited their politics. Father was a somewhat casual Republican, while Mother was a staunch Democrat. Though unable to vote in the presidential election of 1916, Mother left no doubt as to where her sympathies lay. I'm quite certain that her concern influenced Father's vote at that particular time. The cry, "He kept us out of war," was echoed in Hannaford as elsewhere.

I know Mother was shocked when President Wilson, on April 2, 1917, asked Congress for war. Father was convinced that it was necessary. Generally, the people of Hannaford supported the war. The minister of our church defended the war wholeheartedly, denouncing from the pulpit the cruel Hun. The lot of the few German families in the community was not an easy one. Mrs. Schwartz often broke into tears when she confided her fears to Mother. Suspicious neighbors whispered among themselves, and the Schwartz children were taunted and jeered at on the school playground. I was proud of Obie when he stuck up for Reinie Schwartz. Reinie was backed into a corner behind the school toilets and was being shoved and jostled. Reinie did not cringe. His fists were clenched as he shouted, "I am too a good American!" Obie took his place beside Reinie and growled, "A'right, you guys, knock it off." The tormentors faded away when Obie's pal, Ole Thorseth, shouldered his way through the circle.

A town in an adjacent county had a German-born printer who published a weekly newspaper. He had expressed some sympathy for the cause of his homeland in the columns of his little newssheet. Because of this, a gang of unthinking rowdies broke into his print shop and smashed his press.

Jack Wills, after accompanying a carload of cattle to the cities, told of seeing a restaurant menu that listed not wieners and sauerkraut, but wieners and "liberty cabbage." None of the kids in school caught the German measles anymore but rather came down with "liberty" measles. Schools even stopped teaching the German language. German had not been offered in Hannaford, but Latin was taught. Les Larson fervently declared, "I wish we would go to war with the Latins." To such extremes was patriotism carried.

A poster in the Hannaford post office lobby had a stern-looking Uncle Sam saying, "I want you!" We knew that it meant soldiers had to go some place to fight the Germans. We were with Father and Mother at the depot when Uncle Harvey and Uncle Lefty went off to war. We felt mighty proud.

Troop trains frequently stopped in Hannaford so that the steam locomotives could take on coal and water. Sometimes the troops were sailors in navy blue uniforms with white caps and leggings. They would disembark and line up alongside the coaches for calisthenics. At other times we saw doughboys in khaki with wrap leggings and brimmed hats. A leather-lunged drill sergeant would lead them in their exercises, "Wun, two, three, four—up, down, up, down."

The high wooden railroad trestle that spanned the Bald Hill valley was especially vulnerable to destruction by enemy saboteurs. A kind of volunteer home guard undertook the job of patrolling the trestle area. Father took his regular turn and was at times assigned part of the night watch. Equipped with a powerful flashlight, armed with a sawed-off shotgun, and warmly bundled for the night air, Father presented a formidable appearance as he trudged off into the night. No attempts at sabotage were ever made, though Father admitted to a scare during one night patrol. He had distinctly heard sounds of movement in the underbrush along the creek bottom. "Who's there?" he called hoarsely. Increased crackling indicated hurried departure. "Stop! stop—or I'll shoot!" Father ordered. Finally he blasted twice with his buckshot load in the direction of the retreating sounds. His comrades on duty quickly joined him, but a search with a flashlight revealed nothing. The rest of the night passed quietly. Closer inspection by morning light revealed fresh deer tracks in the area.

Father and Mother attended meetings in the schoolhouse and listened to patriotic speeches by "volunteer minutemen." Kids on the street, as well as grownups, hummed, whistled, or sang snatches from such wartime refrains as "Over There," and "You're a Grand Old Flag." When our Aunt Christie took Obie's picture with her marvelous box camera, she posed him standing very straight and holding a small American flag.

A large billboard in the town square proclaimed, "Food Will Win the War." When Mother started to put less sugar into things that she baked and cooked, our dislike of the Germans became even more intense. Del was the loudest protestor at our table about things tasting "sour" or "not tasting like anything." Mother used less white flour in baking, too, and we were not so sure we liked the dark bread that came out of the oven. I don't know how Mother kept track of all of the special eating days. There were "wheatless" Mondays and Wednesdays, "meatless" Tuesdays, and "porkless" Thursdays and Sundays. Obie earnestly told Mother, "It's good that we aren't Catholics, because than we couldn't have meat on Friday either." Mother took pains in explaining to us that there would be more of these things for our soldiers when they reached the French trenches. Del wondered whether Uncle Harvey and Uncle Lefty would have to eat sour applesauce and dark bread wherever they were.

Del really frowned when Mother tacked a poster on our kitchen wall. A smiling child attired in a bib and seated in a high chair was pictured with right hand touching forehead in a snappy military salute. The caption read, "Little Americans, Do Your Bit—

> eat cornmeal mush—oatmeal—corn flakes—
> hominy and rice with milk. Eat no wheat cereals.
> Leave nothing on your plate."

Del's only comment was an exasperated "Oh Boy!"

Mother had always cared for a large garden, but now it became a "victory garden." The song "A Lonesome Little Petunia in an Onion Patch" might well have been written during World War I. The title would certainly have been apt. Potatoes and onions appeared in flower beds and even on boulevards. Mother could not give up all her flowers and a border of her garden remained gay with the bright blooms of poppies, snapdragons, cosmos, nasturtiums, and marigolds. One day, as Mother pulled weeds in her garden, Mr. Wigen passed by on his way home from the bank. He saw fit to chide Mother for wasting valuable victory garden space on flowers. Mother drew herself proudly erect as she replied, "Mr. Wigen, flowers are important to me. I need flowers just as surely as I need the potatoes or onions." Mr. Wigen walked away shaking his head.

Busy mothers somehow found time to spend an afternoon or two a week rolling bandages or knitting socks. Mother didn't profess to be much of a knitter, and apparently she had company. We found it quite hilarious to hear her describe some of the finished footwear. There was a twinkle in Mother's eye as she told of Lizzie Jacobson's heroic efforts. Lizzie was a big woman and she knitted big. According to Mother, only someone of Paul Bunyan size could have filled out Lizzie's socks. Del expressed a longing for a sock of such proportions to challenge Santa Claus with on Christmas Eve.

During the winter and spring many people were struck down with influenza. I know Mother was greatly concerned. If any of her family complained of headache, chills, fever, and aches in the joints, Mother was quick to administer her tried and tested home treatment. A tablespoon of Castoria to clean the bowels, hot mustard foot baths, and plenty of hot lemonade or cocoa to drink was a part of the established torture. Then it was "to bed" for the patient under what seemed like a mountain of heavy quilts. Mother's drastic treatment must have been effective because our household escaped serious flu complications, such as the much feared pneumonia.

Other families did not fare as well; numerous deaths were attributed to the influenza epidemic of 1918–1919. Poor Doc Benson worked unsparingly to care for the stricken, often driving himself to the point of utter exhaustion. The medicines available, even to a physician, were limited, and it was the doctor's mere presence and encouragement that filled the need. The doctor's skill in applying chest poultices and improvising some kind of vapor tent no doubt saved some lives. Doc Benson may not have been jesting when he maintained that he rescued some from being physicked to death.

Though Father's formal schooling ended with sixth grade, he had developed considerable skill along several lines. In the days of steam threshing rigs, he had gained renown all around the Hannaford community as a good grain separator man. A separator man had numerous responsibilities in the threshing operation. First and foremost was to keep the grain separator running smoothly. A breakdown was costly to the owner of the threshing outfit in terms of man power idled and threshing hours lost. A large steam rig might employ upwards of thirty men. Second, a good separator man maintained threshing efficiency, so that valuable grain did not go into the straw pile. Then, too, it was his job to direct the setting and resetting of the machine whenever it was moved to a new location or if the wind shifted direction.

Transient labor made up a goodly part of a threshing crew. During the war, troublemakers, rightly or wrongly identified as IWWs (International Workers of the World—a group that opposed the war), occasionally popped up on the threshing crews. They might encourage a strike, and in isolated cases were even suspected of sabotage of machinery. A box of wooden matches secreted in a bundle of grain could quickly turn a grain separator into a raging inferno.

Father was working as separator man on Uncle Chet's steam threshing rig and witnessed the following incident: Three of the crew (supposedly IWWs) had been trying to stir up trouble for several days. Unable to persuade others to join them in a strike, they announced they were quitting and asked for their time. Uncle Chet, glad to see the last of the trio, paid them off. The troublemakers appeared to be in no hurry to hit the road, but dawdled in the field some distance from the rig. Uncle Chet as usual was back near the steam engine, keeping an eye on the threshing operation, when the ruffians moved determinedly toward him. Whatever mayhem they entertained was cast aside when Uncle Chet casually took a pistol from his pocket and aimed it at a blackbird perched on a nearby grain shock. He fired and the hapless bird flopped to the ground dead. Uncle Chet was scarcely a marksman, but the performance impressed his would-be assailants. They abruptly about-faced and headed for the road leading to town.

With their elders preoccupied with the all-out war effort, the youngsters of Hannaford still found time to play. A sign of the times was the reenactment of trench warfare. Trenches were dug in a weed-choked lot adjacent to our baseball field. The participants in these war games were boys older than we, and we only viewed their mock battles from afar. Their trenches appeared to be about four feet deep, with the excavated dirt thrown up in front.

These aspiring "doughboys" were equipped with nondescript wooden guns, some with bayonets attached. The make-believe "Bang! bang! bang! bang!" might go uninterrupted for some minutes. Then at the cry "Over the top!" the oddly assorted soldiers would attempt the scramble up and over. For some of the shorter-legged this proved an almost insurmountable task. After several unsuccessful jumps, the forepart of the body would hang precariously on the parapet while legs would churn frantically for a kneehold to complete the ascent. The vanguard had pretty well subdued the phantom enemy forces in hand-to-hand combat across no-man's-land before these panting stragglers got to their feet and joined the fray.

The charge across no-man's-land was made more hazardous by several snarls of old barbed wire salvaged from an abandoned fence line. "Fat" Johnson was always the last of the attackers to wiggle his way over the top. At times the victorious Yanks returned to find Fat still struggling with the trench. The barbed wire proved to be Fat's undoing. In his anxious haste to keep pace with his comrades-in-arms, Fat became hopelessly entangled in the barbed wire. The seat of his pants suffered irreparable damage before a rescue squad was able to extricate him. Fat's mother completely demoralized an army that had proved invincible to the Kaiser's finest.

We lesser fry stuck pretty much to our familiar pastimes. Life remained quite tranquil for youngsters growing up on the Bald Hill. There was, of course, no television to bring the war into our living rooms, no radio to give us up-to-the-minute reports. Even the stories carried in daily newspapers suffered a time lag. A Committee on Public Information controlled American thinking on the war. Innocents we were—even children at play—boastfully chanting the jingle:

> Kaiser Bill went up the hill
> To take a look at France.
> Kaiser Bill came down the hill
> With bullets in his pants.

A song sheet of World War I is etched in mind: doughboys, sailors, and marines marching shoulder to shoulder—bayoneted rifles at the ready, forming a protecting shield around a mother and child—and over it all the Stars and Stripes. A part of the lyrics was emblazoned across the artist's cover, "Let's Keep the Glow in Old Glory and the Free in Freedom Too." It may have been corny, but we loved it.

On every hand the people were urged to buy Liberty Bonds. I think it bothered Father that he had little money to lend the government. Ours was, at best, a hand-to-mouth existence. The basic needs of his growing family came first.

Citizens of Hannaford, as elsewhere, enthusiastically ·subscribed to each Liberty Loan campaign. Banker Wigen gave Obie a token medal that could be worn on a watch chain or fob. On the front was stamped the U.S. Treasury building, the American eagle, and the words "Victory Liberty Loan." The back bore this inscription:

> Awarded by the U.S. Treasury Department
> for patriotic service in behalf of
> the Liberty Loans (Made from captured
> German cannon)

On a day in November 1918, the bells of both Hannaford churches began a joyful peal. We knew that it wasn't Sunday. Obie heard the news first. He came tearing home from Thorseth's at full speed. Breathless, he burst in the door to shout, "The war is over!"

Obie, nine; Harvey, seven; Uncle Harvey; Del, five, salute as directed by Uncle Harvey in 1919, during World War I.

Father standing on the grain separator in Uncle Chet's threshing rig.   1918.

Aunt Christie made Obie stand straight when holding the American flag.

We were to learn a day or two later that an armistice had been signed at 11:00 A.M. on November 11, 1918. Up and down the far-flung battlefront the guns fell silent.

Within a few months most of the boys came marching home. Uncle Harvey had served in the Navy and had been assigned to a mine layer. His ship helped lay down mine fields in the North Sea. German U-boats had to negotiate these mined waters to get in or out of their North Sea bases. Uncle Harvey had thrilling tales to tell and snapshots to show us. He lined up Obie, Del, and me in stepladder fashion—each of us standing at attention and giving a military salute—to take our picture. Del got to wear Uncle Harvey's white sailor cap.

Uncle Lefty had been in the Army, but saw no action. He was still in a training camp when the war ended.

In the early 1920s I would spend the summers herding cows on Uncle Chet's farm. Joe Nelson was Uncle Chet's hired man. Joe had suffered shell shock from front-line trench combat. There were nights when he screamed and hollered in his sleep, and I would bury my head beneath a pillow to escape his agonized crying.

One of my most highly prized possessions was a perfectly shaped Indian arrowhead made of a beautiful white flint. I had picked up this treasure out on the prairie while herding cows. Joe greatly admired my find and offered me ten cents for it. I wanted very much to keep the arrowhead, but Joe was my friend and I wanted him to have something special. I knew that he had a terrible hurt inside. Joe had a jeweler attach the arrowhead to his watch chain. It looked very nice displayed on his vest front.

And so the "four longest years in history" reached out even to Hannaford, North Dakota, and left its impression upon a boy growing up on Bald Hill Creek. The war had been a great crusade, but a great disillusionment was its aftermath. Citizens of Hannaford, as elsewhere, were fed up with patriotism and sacrifice and ready to relax, and in 1920 they helped choose a man as president who looked as if he wanted to relax, too.

At least two causes that found favor in Mother's eyes were promoted by the conflict. Mother had always been death against intoxicating liquors. Under the impact of war, sentiment for prohibition mounted rapidly. Brewers were regarded as German-Americans of dubious loyalty, and the use of scarce grain for making alcoholic beverages met with disfavor by those asked to sacrifice and save food. The Eighteenth Amendment became part of the Constitution in 1919.

In 1920 Mother voted for the first time in a presidential election. Male opposition to woman suffrage suddenly crumpled and the Nineteenth Amendment to the Constitution became law in August 1920. I think thereafter that Mother's vote in effect cancelled Father's effort. Mother certainly would have found common ground with Finley Peter Dunne's, Mr. Dooley: "Whin a man gets to be my age, he ducks pol-itical meetin's an' r-reads th' papers and weighs th' ividence an' th' argymints,—pro-argymints an' con-argymints—an' makes up his mind ca'mly, an' votes th' Dimmycratic ticket."

6

Will of the Wind

*A boy's will is the wind's will,/ And the
thoughts of youth are long, long thoughts.*

—LONGFELLOW
"My Lost Youth," 1858.

IF boys growing up on Bald Hill Creek during the 1920s lived venturously, then absence of adult supervision was a virtue wrought of necessity. I know that neither Father nor Mother ever heard us lament, "There's nothing to do." The dawn of each day unveiled untried and devious pathways to explore. We acquired the knowledge of things by doing them. The lessons we learned were sometimes reinforced by the thrill of achievement—oftener by rewards that were painful, including merited chastisement. The thorn of experience often left a memorable imprint.

The inquisitive nature with which boys seem to be endowed often led us to forbidden places and pursuits. Hannaford boasted no garbage pickup service. Each householder was his own garbage man. Trash was piled either in a secluded corner of the backyard or in a convenient ditch. When the pile reached unmanageable proportions or became too malodorous or unsightly it would be hauled to a community dumping ground on the outskirts of town. Haul-out time was usually reserved for spring so that winter's accumulation of ashes could be disposed of along with the trash. These trash piles often yielded treasures dear to our hearts. Broken and discarded toys, worn-out tools, alarm clocks that had ceased ticking, patch-covered rubber inner tubes, and empty tobacco tins were among the salvageable items of junk we lugged home. Mr. Wigen's refuse heap yielded more than its share of such assorted valuables. Often, though, it meant fishing the find out of a mess of potato peelings and other kitchen scraps. Del and I puzzled at length over half shells of grapefruit from the Wigen breakfast table. We knew they were

52

the remains of something edible—and they weren't oranges. Such strange eating habits were a source of amusement to us.

Two old sheds in Lund's backyard served our neighborhood gang as a clubhouse of sorts. One was a low structure with a flat roof. The other had a small loft we could climb into by shinnying up a support post. A window aperture off the loft permitted access onto the flat roof of the adjoining shed. From this vantage point we could survey Mr. Wigen's garden and strawberry patch. If the coast were clear, a quick foray into his oft-guarded preserve provided provisions for our garrison.

Our hideaway under the eaves was guarded zealously. Whenever an intruder did encroach upon our private domain we would make a hasty but guarded exit by the roof route. From a precarious hanging handhold on the lower edge we could drop to the ground and disappear into the leafy jungle of Mr. Wigen's trees. Mother never could quite figure out why the sheds were always empty. Some sixth sense mothers seem to have would lead her there when we either didn't hear or didn't heed her summoning call.

The summer sun beating upon the roof made our inner sanctum stiflingly hot and quite untenable. On rainy days it proved an especially delightful retreat. The soft patter of raindrops on the moss-grown wooden shingles overhead made each assembled lad a philosopher profound. Flights of fancy took us to far-off places. Del loved to recline on his stomach with upper body propped on elbows and upturned heels moving in rhythmic pattern. Of more practical bent than most, his thoughts turned easily to the garden edibles close by. For all, the fantasy would pass and idle hands would seek new pursuits—sometimes questionable.

It was perhaps inevitable that early attempts at smoking were made within the murky confines of our shelter. Real tobacco was hard to come by, and we experimented with some rather dubious substitutes. Dried willow leaves had the color of tobacco, but beyond that, any resemblance was but a figment of youthful imagination. Nonetheless, we crumbled the stuff into usable form and stuffed it into discarded Bull Durham sacks. It certainly gave a fellow a feeling of man's estate to carry one of these little cloth sacks in the bib pocket of his overalls, with the drawstring tab dangling prominently over the pocket edge. The thinnest pages we could glean from the outhouse store of old mail-order catalogs and matches filched from the kitchen matchbox holder completed our smoking equipment.

Each would-be smoker rolled his own, and the ludicrous finished products seemed somehow to mirror personality. Del's effort invariably resulted in an outsized, lumpy stogie that even heroic applications of spit could scarce hold together. Obie's cigarette, on the other hand, looked as a cigarette should, slender, firm, and very proper. Since paper was neither measured nor cut, but torn off to suit individual fancy, the lengths of the smokes varied, as did the girths. There were stubs, regulars, king-size, as well as extra-longs.

Light-up time was almost ceremonial. We would all wait deferentially for Obie to strike the first match. This he would attempt with a flourish not always successful. More often than not, the tries on the seat of his pants failed. Sometimes he scratched so hard and furiously that the matchstick would break. If by chance he wore shoes, he might deign to strike the match on an upturned sole. If barefooted, he would bow to the inevitable and ignominiously scratch the match on the nearest piece of wood.

The lighted match would be held for each smoker in turn or until it burned Obie's fingers. Del was the first to master the trick of igniting a match with a flick of the thumbnail. Obie relinquished his role as lighter with considerably bad grace.

Contented puffing and exclamations of feigned pleasure soon gave way to bursts of coughing and undisguised dismay, as the acrid smoke irritated eyes and throats. I remember well one such occasion. Clouds of stinging smoke swirled and eddied in the confines of the loft. Finally it almost obscured vision. Placid Del started the mad scramble toward the window exit and fresh air. He and Obie tried to squeeze through at the same time. Del was quite sturdily built around the rear and momentarily the two were stuck. The rest of us, now gagging in the choking smudge within, pushed desperately. We didn't know that the seat of Obie's pants was caught fast on a nail. There was a distinct ripping sound as the stout denim gave way, and we all tumbled out on the adjoining roof together.

For several minutes no one noticed Obie's plight. We lay there gasping and coughing and blinking tears from smarting eyes. Finally Bumpy's unbelieving voice, "Obie, your overalls—the back is gone." We stared in disbelief. There he was, his naked bottom quite exposed, the tattered remains of overalls, held by suspenders, hung like an apron down his front. The entire back of Obie's overalls adorned the loft window frame.

Disenchantment with willow leaves failed to dissuade us from our determination to smoke. The prairie abounded with what we called Indian tobacco. The ripened seed top of this wild plant, when stripped off, looked very much like a fine-cut pipe tobacco. Again the empty Bull Durham sack or an empty Prince Albert tin served as container for this ersatz tobacco. Though Indian tobacco looked more like the real thing than did the willow leaf, its smoking qualities were little better and not apt to addict anyone. We found more fulfillment in the gathering and possession of Indian tobacco than in the actual smoking of it.

The dried stalks of pigweeds made fine cheroots when cut into proper lengths. The pith in the center of the stem was porous enough for drawing the smoke through, but didn't burn too well, and furious puffing was required to keep the things lit. The smoke from these delights was hot and biting and a few puffs made nonsmoking respectable again—at least until the next time.

We all envied Joe Kohler his battered corncob pipe. Joe was labeled by teachers a slow-witted boy and had come to be regarded the town tough. Whether found or purloined, the pipe gave Joe an aura of worldliness we much envied. Joe was abruptly and rudely reduced to earthly stature when Bill Ferris discovered him smoking his pipe in the Ferris barn. Mr. Ferris had got a whiff of something burning as he entered the hay-filled building. Alarmed, he made a hurried search and discovered Joe lolling in a corner of the haymow puffing contentedly on his corncob. Joe was hauled unceremoniously out by the scruff of his neck and the seat of his pants. Upon examining Joe's pipe, Mr. Ferris was flabbergasted to find that the smouldering stuff in the bowl was cotton string. Our awe of Joe diminished considerably after that. After all, who but a sissy would stoop to smoking string? Needless to say, the Bill Ferris farm was off limits for Joe from that time on.

Bud Jackson was a couple of years younger than I, but living next door made him an acceptable associate at times. Bud was slightly built and on the delicate order, so he did not always participate in our rough-and-tumble games. At times we may have used Bud unfairly. Eager to ingratiate himself, he could always be prevailed upon to raid his mother's kitchen for cookies and other goodies. Too bashful myself to ask the Alm twins to join us for sledding or games, I would prevail upon Bud to go to their door and knock. From a secure position behind a tree, I would watch as Bud asked if the girls could come out. If his mission proved successful, Bud himself was all but forgotten in the ensuing play.

Mr. Jackson had a small garage for his Model T Ford. It stood some distance from the Jackson house in a corner of their yard and adjoining our garden. Mr. Jackson kept the doors to the garage locked when not using the car. One wet rainy day, Bud and I, along with several of the neighborhood gang, found the door unlocked and entered to escape the drizzle without. A long-disused deer rifle hung on the wall. Dust and cobwebs festooned the weapon. Being the oldest one in the group that day, I led the way in examining the items stored in the garage. Ignoring Bud's apparent consternation, I gingerly lifted the heavy gun from its place on the wall. I could scarcely lift it to sight down the long, cumbersome octagonal barrel. The rusty lever action worked under protest. The first time I pulled the trigger the hammer clicked harmlessly on an empty chamber. The second time there was a deafening explosion. The breech of the firearm burst almost in my face. Bud screamed and clapped his hands over his ears. The blast might have ruptured his eardrums. Ashen-faced, for some minutes we could only stand and stare. We were frozen in shocked surprise. Miraculously no one was hurt. The bullet had lodged in the rusted rifling of the barrel.

Mr. Jackson was mortified beyond words that his all-but-forgotten old hunting rifle should have been left there to tempt. Father lectured at length on the ever-present danger of the "unloaded" gun. I'm certain this alarming episode taught those of us involved an invaluable lesson about the handling of firearms. When Obie later obtained a .22-calibre repeating rifle from Uncle Lefty, he shared its use with Del, Bumpy, and me. We used it safely and without incident on many a safari along Bald Hill Creek. The same care and caution prevailed in our use of the old Winchester 12-gauge repeating shotgun that Grandpa Rasmussen entrusted to us.

Summer thunderstorms frequently shattered the tranquility of a quiet, peaceful day on the Dakota prairie. Sharp bolts of lightning and window-rattling crashes of thunder were frightening in themselves, but it was the wind that Mother dreaded. She was quick to herd her brood to the basement whenever the sky threatened. Father often scoffed at her concern. He could sleep right through the wildest tumult unless awakened by anxious Mother. Very early one threatening morning, Mother had deemed it necessary to rouse Father. The early morning sky had a distinctly ominous look. A sleepy, grumbling Father was pulling on his pants when the wind hit. Peering out from an upstairs window we saw that the small barn housing Old Dan, our buggy horse, was teetering precariously on sharply tilted edge. The only thing that kept the flimsy shed from being blown away was a bending, gyrating tree against which it was pressed. Father grabbed his raincoat and ran barefooted into the storm. Ducking underneath the upraised side of the building, Father managed to cut the straining halter rope that held Old Dan a prisoner. Moments later the barn went rolling, but Father and the horse emerged unscathed.

Matt Benson, a bachelor neighbor, lived alone in a rather flimsy shack. When a cyclone threatened he would join us in the relative safety of our cellar. Matt was scarcely a comfort to any of us. As the storm crashed overhead and the house creaked on its foundation, Matt would cock his head upward and regale us with his chilling pronouncements of impending doom: "The house is gonna go now! Listen! It's gonna go! Here it goes! Was that ever close! It's coming again now—now it will go!"

Over a period of several such experiences we become accustomed to Matt's ominous predictions and each time vowed to ignore them in future emergencies. Nonetheless, each subsequent performance would find us shivering anew.

The heavy downpour of rain that usually accompanied summer thunderstorms left ditches overflowing. Some of these ditches were far too deep to wade in and we were challenged to build rafts with which to negotiate them. We usually found enough old boards and posts to fashion a floating craft of sorts. Some of the rafts proved less than seaworthy, especially if overloaded. A near disaster occurred when Del and I were navigating alone one day. We were poling our rather unstable platform in a newly excavated ditch when Del decided to disembark. His side of the raft was close enough to the edge of the road so that he could safely jump to shore. My station on the far side paralleled the center and deepest part of the canal. Del's sudden departure rocked the tottery raft and I was unceremoniously dumped into the roily water. It may have been five or six feet deep at the point where I submerged. The sudden release of my weight caused the raft to lurch over me, and my head bumped its underside as I tried to surface. Momentarily I panicked and found myself struggling blindly in the murky depths. Calmer reasoning came to my rescue. I swam underwater away from the ponderous deck overhead and emerged blowing and sputtering. Del found my predicament delightful and was guffawing with glee. He somehow managed to contain his mirth long enough to give me a hand in scrambling up the slippery bank. " 'Taint funny, Del," I rasped, "I coulda drowned in there." I don't think that possibility had entered Del's head at all. His was the confidence on water of one practically born to swimming.

In the early 1920s, free movies were shown on the main street of Hannaford every Saturday night during the summer. Since it didn't get dark until nine or ten o'clock, people had ample time to do their shopping before the show started. The silent pictures were projected from an upstairs window of the town's movie hall onto the wall of a lumberyard shed across the street. At each showing the street was jammed to its full width with automobiles backed into position facing this improvised screen. Those without a car sat on benches or the curb, or stood, as fancy suited. Kids perched everywhere—on the hoods or tops of cars, on steps of outside stairways, on rooftops, and even in convenient tree crotches.

Invariably the show began with lantern slides advertising the wares of local businesses. A slapstick comedy came next. The enthusiastic audience roared at the antics of "The Tramp" as portrayed by Charlie Chaplin and at the wild chases of The Keystone Cops. Other favorite comedians were stony-faced Buster Keaton and cross-eyed Ben Turpin. After the comedy came the feature. This was the silent era of the 1920s and the black-and-white picture was accompanied by piano music. The piano was located on a convenient loading platform of the lumber shed. Dialogue had to be read from titles printed on the film. There was never a dearth of readers. Always someone in your viewing vicinity had to read aloud the captions before he or she could react. This could prove quite an irritation to those a step ahead in the struggle to interpret the story. There was no such thing as simultaneous reaction by the viewing audience.

Father was a quite indifferent viewer of the picture shows and could seldom either sit or stand through the entire feature. One of the few pictures that he waxed enthusiastic over was *The Three Musketeers,* a swashbuckling adventure story starring Douglas Fairbanks. Feature-length comedies with shy Harold Lloyd he could tolerate.

Since our family automobile was seldom operational, Mother rarely took in the free Saturday night movies. She considered it unladylike to sit on the curb and found it tiring to stand. The calendar picture of Mary Pickford, "America's Sweetheart," that graced her bedroom wall indicated Mother's preference among the stars of the period. She doubtless shared, along with millions of other women, a secret heartthrob for the great lover of the silent screen, Rudolph Valentino. In later years we enjoyed teasing her as to what prompted her to select Rudolph as a middle name for her youngest son. Mother never could satisfactorily explain her choice. To our knowledge there was no Rudolph on either side of our family lineage.

Next to the comedies and rip-roaring adventure stories, my pals and I liked the westerns. Our cowboy favorites were William S. Hart and Tom Mix, and we galloped many a dusty mile with these straight-shooting good guys.

Toward fall, when the evenings became uncomfortably cold for outdoor movies, the show was moved into the low-ceilinged community hall. Here seating was at a premium and with all of the chairs on floor level, only assiduous neck craning enabled viewers beyond the very front rows to enjoy much of the picture. Only the small fry, from their up-front vantage point, enjoyed unobstructed view of the small screen. The unceasing piano accompaniment drowned out the noise of the youngsters. The pianist of the silent movie era had a challenging job, always trying to match the mood of her music to the prevailing vein of emotion portrayed on the screen.

Del and I were so moved by the epic World War I picture, *Lilac Time,* that we sat through it twice. The story was of American pilots of the Lafayette Escadrille participating in the aerial warfare over the battle lines. These devil-may-care airmen went out day after day seeking enemy planes and trying to destroy them in dogfights. Some of their battles involved a number of aircraft at once, a swirling melee in full view of the ground troops in the trenches below. The ranks of these swashbuckling air warriors were reduced almost daily as Allied planes fell to the skill of the German aces. The survivors toasted their missing comrades and flew forth again to challenge and avenge. Del and I thrilled at their bravado. One of these intrepid heroes took off on what proved to be his last mission with the silk stocking of his companion of the night before knotted gaily around his neck.

Airplanes improved tremendously during World War I and came of age during the 1920s and early 1930s. How well I remember the first airplane that appeared over Hannaford. A neighborhood baseball game was in progress when it happened. From his right field vantage point atop the manure pile, Peasoup saw it first.

Harvey's wooden rendition of the Spirit of St. Louis.

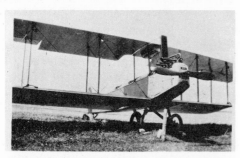

The first airplane that flew over Hannaford. 1920.

Astonishment rendered him speechless and he could only jump up and down and point. An awe-struck Ole hollered, "He landed in the field beyond the depot."

Game forgotten, a mad scramble in that direction ensued. There it stood in all its glory—an open-cockpit biplane—a 1918 vintage Curtiss Jenny. The pilot had made an emergency landing because he was low on gas. The plane was pushed up to a fence line and securely tied down. The pilot stayed in Hannaford overnight until suitable fuel for the plane was obtained. Through the open windows of our schoolroom we heard him take off the next morning.

From then on, an occasional airplane would fly over Hannaford. Always these brief appearances elicited excitement, and citizens would run out and crane necks skyward. The 4th of July, 1925, was a memorable one in that a barnstorming pilot offered rides throughout the day. He used a level part of Bill Ferris's pasture for his airfield. He took a single passenger at a time for a few wide circles over Hannaford and the countryside. We were all surprised that day when Del announced his determination to take an airplane ride. He had the five dollar fare and was willing to part with it for the anticipated sky venture. Pride in his venturesome son assured Father's approval. Mother expressed considerable trepidation, but finally gave her reluctant consent.

I'm sure we all entertained some degree of misgiving as Del was buckled into the open forward cockpit. He strove mightily to be nonchalant about the whole thing, even attempting a halfhearted wave as the pilot taxied the machine to the take-off point. The unnatural pallor of his face belied Del's front of bravery.

The careening machine became airborne in a cloud of dust. Throughout the brief flight, our eyes were glued to the circling plane. Del got his money's worth. On one of his passes over the pasture airfield the pilot made a rather steep dive, followed by a zooming climb right overhead. His line of flight in that maneuver was low enough so that we could make out Del's white, stricken face over the edge of the cockpit.

Mother gave an audible sigh of relief when the flight ended. A rather wobbly Del clambered down to the ground. Surrounded by a questioning throng of admirers, Del soon regained his composure and made the most of his moment of triumph. "Sure I liked it!" he declared. "Naw, I wasn't scared—the dive was fun! Sure, I'd go again—if I had the money." Basking in the hero's role, Del waxed eloquent. "Boy did everything look little from up there. I could see our house. It looked like a matchbox. People and cars were like ants. The crick looked like a winding little ditch." Del's head remained in the clouds for several days. Maybe I was a little envious. In my heart I admired Del's pluck. I'm not at all certain I could have nerved myself to go up that day.

Citizens of Hannaford were thrilled, as were millions of people around the world, when an American aviator made the first solo flight across the Atlantic Ocean. On a May morning in 1927 I heard drayman Frank Olson shout out the news, "He made it!" I knew that "he" was Charles Lindbergh.

Later that summer I painstakingly fashioned a wooden model of The Spirit of St. Louis. It looked quite realistic and with it I was able to perpetrate a hoax on Ole Thorseth. I hung the model by a thread from Mother's clothesline and then used my little box camera to snap a picture of it from an underneath, oblique angle. The resulting picture was a dandy. The airplane appeared to be in flight over neighbor Larson's house. Ole was taken in completely. "When did it go over?" he asked plaintively. "Did it land?" When Obie decided to set the record straight and spilled the beans to his pal, Ole's discomfiture at being hoodwinked was evident. Ole tried to save the day by pretending he knew all along that my picture was a fake. Most of us knew better.

The interest in aircraft and flight led to a fever of kite building the like of which Hannaford had never seen. I probably built and flew more kites than any other kid in town. My creations were all of simple, pretty much standard design, a light diamond-shaped framework of slat and string covered with paper. Knotted strips of cloth formed the tail, which was fastened to the lower end of the kite and served to steady it in flight. Quite often, when the last bundle of grain was cut and bound in the fall, some twine would be left in the grain binder. Kite-minded boys would not hesitate to visit the stored binders and appropriate the partly used balls of twine. More than likely the old twine would have been removed and discarded at the start of a new harvesting season anyway. What better use could it possibly serve than helping a boy to advance in the art of kite sailing? Binder twine was a very strong thread of several strands of jute twisted together. Its one disadvantage was its weight. A kite at the end of 500 or 600 feet of binder twine was held down considerably by the combined weight of twine and tail. In fact, only a stout wind would keep it airborne.

Kite marathons paralleled the numerous attempts at long-distance airplane flight that followed Lindbergh's successful

Atlantic crossing. We competed to see whose kite could remain in flight the longest. The sturdy paper lining the railroad boxcars used for shipping grain reinforced our kites for these endurance contests. A sustained wind might keep a kite in the air overnight. This meant anchoring it to a fence post or utility pole at bedtime and trusting that a shifting or dying wind would not lodge it in a tree or tangle it around a church steeple. A three-day March gale from a prevailing northerly direction helped me set an unbeaten record of a shade over fifty-one hours. The whipping tail of my battered kite finally became entangled in a treetop. Intermittent flurries of rain mixed with snow had dampened but not grounded my sturdy voyageur. A half-dozen messages from the ground had been sent up to encourage the imaginary crew. A small cardboard disk with a hole cut in the center and windmill vanes radiating outward would be slipped over the free end of the kite twine. Whirled and propelled upward along the string by the wind, the communication would take only minutes to reach the kite.

A dispirited Del, with the endurance record beyond reach, set to work to build a box kite. His kite consisted of two almost square boxes, open on both ends. He covered the intricate frame with some bright blue-and-white striped gingham salvaged from Mother's old apron. His box kite required no tail to weight it down and flown from a light wrapping string it soared to prodigious heights. It was truly a thing of beauty in flight, floating gracefully and smoothly on even a light breeze. Del's masterpiece was in a class by itself and his spirits soared with it. He had redeemed himself.

A boy's kite caught fast in a tree
With tattered paper and tangled string,
In vain his efforts to set it free—
Upward again it will never fling.

But kites like dreams will be built anew
And successfully launched, and it would seem
That man's future is his will to do,
For you can't destroy a dream.

—HARVEY SLETTEN, "Kites and Dreams," 1956

7

Lizzie and Mother Had to Jump

"THE one who first realized the usefulness of things that rolled and who invented the wheel was one smart gent." Del ventured this astute observation as he hammered the nails that would attach a set of wheels to the underside of his racy looking pushmobile. The assembled onlookers, including myself, were in hearty agreement. The wheels, with their narrow tires of hard rubber, and the axle to which they were attached had been salvaged from a junked baby carriage.

Our boyish fascination for wheels was reflected in many of our pursuits. Discarded alarm clocks were eagerly sought, and whenever a neighborhood trash pile yielded one, it was a red-letter day. Mother's kitchen table became the workshop. The first task was to remove the clock's works from its case. Repair of the clock as a timekeeper was not our purpose. Rather, it was the motive power of the inner mechanism that we sought to harness. Of immediate concern was the mainspring. If that was intact, we had our motor. The balance wheel with attached hairspring was carefully removed. This permitted the rest of the wheels to turn unimpeded. The toothed wheel that motivated the balance wheel would also be removed and set on a longer axle. A section of a steel sewing needle served nicely for this purpose. With a wooden pulley mounted on the extended shaft, the clock's works had been transformed into an engine. Empty wooden spools that had held Mother's sewing thread became pulleys for all kinds of make-believe machines. Drive belts of string turned our wheels of industry—sawmill, threshing rig, whatever an eager boy's fancy dictated.

Every red-blooded boy in Hannaford had mastered the art of hoop rolling before he ever started school. For our particular type of hoop rolling we used the iron rim from the wooden wheel of a toy coaster wagon. Such a band, from eight to twelve inches in diameter, was ideal. A hoop stick was an inverted T made from lath and cut to a length to accomodate the size of the boy behind it. The handle was carefully smoothed and shaped to fit the owner's hand. A well-rounded iron rim of desired thickness and size was hard to come by, and once found, was carefully guarded.

A spinning, bounding hoop pursued by a running, barefooted boy was a common sight on the dusty paths and tired sidewalks of Hannaford. One could not tarry when following a rolling hoop. If the operator slowed his pace to a walk, the hoop would wobble and die in its track. It took momentum to keep it rolling smoothly ahead. A sudden stop required a quick maneuver with the hoop stick to spear the darting rim before it became a runaway.

Rolling a hoop did have its own peculiar hazards. Guiding the flashing wheel along a tortuous path at a dead run could lead to unexpected encounters. A suspiciously moist slipperiness underfoot led to painful awareness that a cow fresh from green pastures had preceded you up that pathway. Or skimming along an uneven sidewalk with its often depressed and broken squares could result in a badly stubbed toe.

Regardless of these perils the hoops rolled, rain or shine, even after the first light snowfalls. Mother knew that an errand to the store was speedily accomplished by a boy chasing a hoop. If one of us were tardy in volunteering his services or exhibited a degree of reluctance, Mother would achieve her purpose by artfully suggesting, "Why don't you take your hoop?" There was, of course, a limit to what a boy could carry in his one free arm while propelling a hoop. Mother sensed these limits and when more than a small item was needed would suggest "driving" our battered old coaster wagon. It must have been sturdily built, for it somehow survived the punishing use bestowed by four exuberant boys. It was only retired when its wobbly wheels finally disintegrated under Bumpy's grueling regime. He was the last to inherit it.

Hand-me-downs were Bumpy's lot as the youngest of Mother's marauders. Beat-up playthings he cheerfully accepted. He may have been somewhat less enthusiastic over the articles of clothing he "grew into" as Del "grew out of" them. Mother made our dress outfits, complete with ruffled shirts and knee-bottom pants. At the tender ages that may have extended until we were eight or ten, the pants were constructed without a fly. This made the front and the rear quite indistinguishable. They bagged on both sides and Del once complained, "Kids ask me if I've got my pants on backwards."

Even Mother was hard pressed for an answer when one Sunday

morning, as she prepared to help Bumpy into a pair of Del's "grown out of" pants, Bumpy ventured a mild protest, "Why can't I get the new clothes sometime and let Del wear my hand-me-ups?"

One of the few playthings that Bumpy enjoyed in a brand new state was a wooden kiddie-car Father brought home for him one day. Bumpy and that kiddie-car were inseparable until he outgrew it and graduated to the coaster wagon. Bumpy was built quite close to the ground and he had to be content to pull the wagon until his stubby legs lengthened enough to permit coasting, with one knee riding the wagon and the other leg propelling. That coaster wagon was at times a steam locomotive pulling a string of passenger-laden coaches. At other times it became a covered wagon crossing Indian-infested prairies on the long trek west.

Tina was granted occasional rides in the wagon. She became increasingly leery of this privilege after an exuberant Bumpy failed to negotiate a corner at high speed and overturned the wagon, sending Tina sprawling in the roadway. Tina had her own coterie of playmates. Two of them had scooters, and indulgent Father decided that a scooter was probably a safer vehicle for Tina than coaster wagons propelled in helter-skelter fashion by rambunctious drivers.

Tina's scooter consisted of a narrow board mounted on two wheels, tandem, and was guided by means of a handle attached to the front wheel. Tina stood with one foot on the board and pushed with the other. She became quite adept in using it, racing up and down the sidewalk in a manner that Bumpy and Del might have envied. Father firmly discouraged their using it, however, making clear that it was a child's vehicle and not built to stand up under the rugged abuse they would, of a certainty, give it.

Our excitement knew no bounds when Obie proudly rode a bicycle into our yard. He managed to dodge the overturned coaster wagon, Bumpy's kiddie-car, the horseshoe stakes, and Del's wooden stilts before he grandly dismounted near the kitchen steps. Obie tried to sound casual as he announced that he had bought it for five dollars—that it was truly his. Del and I were speechless. We could only walk around and around it, admiring. It was in no way a fancy wheel. The red paint was worn off in spots and the front wheel was warped enough that the tire rubbed on the steering fork. In our eyes the defects were minor. Almost unbelievable was the fact that the cycle belonged to Obie—and indirectly to us. Obie was pretty good at sharing.

Our bicycle was a vintage model of undetermined age, definitely pre–World War I. It had been a trade-in of dubious value at the Thorseth Hardware Store. Mr. Thorseth was glad to let it go for five dollars, with his blessing thrown in. Both wheels were the same size and it did have pneumatic tires. Our ancient machine antedated the coaster brake; you slowed by exerting back pressure on the pedals or by an agile dismount. It had neither mudguards nor chain guard. Riding it on a wet or muddy street could be a traumatic experience. Even a short sortie under such conditions left a thoroughly bespattered rider. Del tried running behind it when Obie rode on the first wet day. It happened that Del had on his Sunday shirt and pants. Mother shook her head in despair when the speckled apparition, who a few minutes before had been immaculate, made a bedraggled appearance.

That lowly but sturdy wheel was the only bicycle we had as boys. It served the four of us faithfully, though it did require yeoman's service to keep it operational. Broken and battered wire wheel spokes were replaced as needed. We learned to use a spoke-tightening wrench to keep the wheels reasonably straight. The rubber tires were single tubes that had to hold air, cling to the rim, and also cling to the road. These single-tube tires were cemented on the wooden rims. If punctured, they were difficult to repair. A rubber sealer squeezed into the puncture might stop the air leak for awhile. If we didn't have a tube of sealer, we simply wrapped black friction tape tightly around the tube. This was not a very durable repair as road friction would quickly reduce the tape to tatters.

The unguarded drive chain was an ever-present hazard to the rider's pants leg if he attempted to ride without a pants guard. The pants guard was a simple metal clip of light spring steel that was placed around the lower part of the right trouser leg to keep it out of the moving chain. A pants leg caught between the chain and the pedal sprocket wheel not only chewed up the pants leg but could conceivably cause leg injury or a disastrous spill.

The drive chain would sometimes break, as constant wear weakened the links. Spare links were available at the hardware store. Prying or pounding off the ends of the broken link took some doing. Once that was accomplished, the repair link could be snapped into place with a pliers. At times the oft-repaired chain became too loose and might jump from the sprockets and jam up spokes in the rear wheel.

Despite its many drawbacks, that battered bicycle holds a cherished place in the happy memories of four boys. We managed to share its use with a minimum of bickering. Obie, of course, had first claim to riding the bicycle and he was also the head mechanic on

Mr. and Mrs. Albin Larson owned their own motorcycle in the early 1920s. Even Mother wanted to ride such a machine.

Bumpy had his very own wheels—a kiddie car. 1920.

Tina (left) and a couple of her friends with their scooters and wooden wagon in 1927.

Bumpy and friend Doug Reite in 1924. That wheel served all four of us boys faithfully.

Del and Obie, 1918. Our pants were made by Mother, alike in front and back with no flys.

Harvey, Del, and Obie, 1916, models for Mother's homemade fashions.

what seemed incessant repair work. He grumbled a bit at times that Del and I were hard on the cycle—almost as though we banged it up on purpose. At times Obie rode the bike out to Grandpa Rasmussen's farm, a distance of more than ten miles over rough and dusty roads. Fortunately most of the journey was over fairly level terrain. That bike pedalled hard, and going up even a slight incline was a test of a boy's endurance. On steeper grades the rider would dismount and push the wheel to the top of the rise.

At times we bicycled to the swimming hole below town. Two of us would attempt to ride tandem, one doing the pedalling and steering, the other perched precariously on the crossbar. Usually, we were off to a wobbly start, with some doubts entertained by the passenger as to the wisdom of electing to ride double. The descent down the hill to the creek below was a madcap experience. As the force of gravity took over, all that we could do was hang on and steer. It was useless to try to brake. With our cotton bathing suits flapping wildly from the handlebars, we bounced across the little wooden bridge over the creek and slithered off the road onto the path that ended at the bathhouses. More than once, as Del dismounted at the end of the wild ride, he would state with finality, "Harvey that is the last time I ever ride double with you."

On the homeward trek we had to walk and push the wheel all the way up the long hill. That was the time that tried boys' souls. Del would suddenly become very, very tired—too tired to take his turn at pushing. Hot words were sometimes exchanged. As we neared the top and if Del happened to lag a little bit behind, I would summon a last bit of strength and push on the run. Once on level ground, I would make a flying mount and ride off, leaving Del behind screaming his protest.

We were much impressed and envious when a new boy came to town and started to ride his motorcycle. His was the first engine-driven bicycle to appear in Hannaford. The year was 1925. A belt running from the engine to the rear wheel supplied the power. The new boy's name, we learned, was Haakon Stubskjoen. "Stub" seemed natural and desirable as a nickname. Stub's machine could "putt-putt" up the creek hill with a little running start to overcome belt slippage. It was downright humiliating to have Stub "ride" by us as we struggled up the hill pushing our wheel.

Even Mother expressed admiration for Stub's motorcycle and often admitted a secret desire to ride such a machine. She had shown us that she could ride a bicycle. We had been a bit skeptical of her claims to prowess as a cyclist. Whenever we challenged her to ride our wheel, she had always avoided our dare by pleading the difficulty imposed by her long skirt. Then a cousin of Mother's came to visit and brought with her a riding habit of sorts. It consisted of a white middy and voluminous, knee-length black bloomers.

Mother startled us all by donning this rakish apparel and announcing her intention to go bicycling. Needless to say we all trooped outside to the yard to watch. After a first abortive attempt in which she and the machine almost did a cropper, Mother's triumphant ride began. She steered an erratic course across our pathworn yard, down through a fortunately shallow ditch, and up onto the dirt roadway. Mr. Wigen had chosen that moment to drive up the street in his stately Model T sedan. Mother's sudden appearance on the road so surprised him that he momentarily lost control of his car. Turning too sharply, he missed his driveway by a couple of feet and bounced across the protruding end of a metal culvert. Unruffled, Mother cruised to the end of the block, executed a hairpin turn, and made a triumphal return. Bumpy led the cheer of heartfelt admiration for our intrepid Mother. From the safety of his own yard, Mr. Wigen shook his head in apparent wonderment and disbelief.

Lizzie Jacobson was a frequent visitor at our house. Despite somewhat different temperaments, she and Mother were good friends. Lizzie was quite positive in her likes and dislikes. She evidenced no great fondness for children and made clear that she believed they should be seen and not heard. We had learned to remain discreetly silent in her presence. Del could ill conceal his dislike for Lizzie, and Mother fully expected that he would show it. I think this is why we were encouraged to play outdoors whenever Lizzie visited. The two women had this in common: they were both strong willed, and sometimes they argued vehemently. Father usually remembered unfinished business or pressing engagements elsewhere whenever Lizzie barged in.

Lizzie's constant companion was her dog, Bumpsie. Though Mother had no marked fondness for dogs, she had learned to tolerate Bumpsie. If you valued Lizzie's friendship, you accepted Bumpsie. It was that simple. Where Lizzie went, there also went Bumpsie. Bumpsie was a nondescript dog, a large ungainly animal with a tightly kinked, curly black coat. A trace of white marking appeared just above the nose, on the chest, and on the tip of his tail.

Lizzie highly regarded Bumpsie's merits as a watchdog. Lizzie lived alone and felt quite secure in her belief that Bumpsie's barking and growling would frighten away burglars and safeguard her home and property.

To us children, Bumpsie was a good-natured clown, and we believed that like his mistress, the bark was worse than the bite.

One night we had occasion to see this vaunted guardian of home and hearth in action. On this particular evening, Lizzie and Mother occupied our living room, with Lizzie comfortably ensconced in Father's big rocking chair. She knitted as she rocked and visited. Bumpsie sprawled on a scatter rug at her feet and snored softly.

Pranksters had been knocking at our front door and scurrying away to hide before Mother could answer the knock. Patient Mother was willing to ignore the annoyance, knowing that the funsters would soon tire of their little game.

Not so, Lizzie. Ignoring Mother's protest, she stationed her portly self near the door and urged the languid Bumpsie into wakeful vigilance. When the knock was repeated, Lizzie yanked open the door and bade the dog, "Sick 'em Bumpsie!"

With a throaty growl Bumpsie launched his bulk into the darkness beyond the door. His attack stopped short of his quarry, and in the dim light we saw his tail start to wag. A boyish voice in the darkness exclaimed, "Why it's only good ol' Bumpsie!"

Mother's eyes danced with concealed amusement as an embarrassed Lizzie ordered Bumpsie back into the house. Del practically hooted in delight as he playfully pummeled "good ol'" Bumpsie."

I felt the brunt of Lizzie's wrath on a peaceful summer evening when she and I had a near collision. We had not had our bicycle very long, and I was enjoying riding it around and around the block. My proficiency as a cyclist at that stage left something to be desired. The exhilaration of learning to ride was a heady wine, and I may never have been as elated and excited.

Mother, Lizzie, and Bumpsie were returning from a quiet stroll in the twilight when I raced toward them. With reckless bravado, I was intent on showing off my newly acquired skill. I firmly intended to execute a flying dismount right in front of the unexpecting trio. Unfortunately, I misjudged both my speed and the intervening distance. There was no way I could stop the careening machine. The startled ladies froze in their tracks as the apparition bore down upon them. A chain fence bordered the sidewalk on the inner side, and extending well over to it was Lizzie—no chance to bypass there. On Mother's side were the ditch and Bumpsie. A split-second decision favored Mother's agility over the immovable object. A desperate last-minute swerve toppled me and the bicycle into the ditch.

A solicitous Mother was reassured as to my well-being when I sat up and managed a sheepish grin. She only then turned to help free an irate Lizzie, whose bustle was caught fast in the fence. "Lan' sakes," sputtered the flustered woman, "that boy deserves a sound spanking, riding his bicycle up the sidewalk like that and just about running over a body!"

Good ol' Bumpsie let me know that he held no grudge. He sat beside me in the ditch and licked my face.

8

Father's Shotgun Went "Poof"

ALMOST overnight, the leaves of the poplar, so anxiously watched for growth in the spring, were turning color. A bright October morning, with the season's first white frost sparkling on the grass, might find me scooting, still barefoot, on an errand to the store. My reluctance to don shoes at summer's end was a source of some concern to Mother. Half-scoldingly she would say, "People will think that you don't have shoes."

I guess my brothers and I had mixed feelings about fall. The swimming hole below town was now deserted. Only a muskrat, busily garnering his winter stores, rippled the placid water. A forgotten bathing suit flapped forlornly beneath the springboard.

Games of one o'cat, work-up, and choose-up gave way to our own tumultuous version of football. It was a rough-and-tumble affair and had a ruinous effect on clothes and shoes. For Mother it was a seasonal catastrophe to be endured. We played with a bloated, out-of-shape football, which often became deflated in the middle of a heated contest. Action would be halted while Obie and Ole removed the rubber innards and added yet another patch.

The tang of fall in the air spurred on preparations for winter. The many and varied tasks involved the entire family. Even Tina would join Bumpy and Del in picking up potatoes as Father and Obie unearthed them with digging forks. My task was to haul them home, a sackful at a time, in a sturdy play wagon. They were stored in a partitioned bin in the earth-walled cellar alongside Mother's now-bulging shelves of summer's canning. Meanwhile, Mother might be lifting and topping remaining beets and carrots. The freshly dug carrots were stored between layers of sand in a large earthen crock.

Later in the fall or early winter Father would add a large

wooden barrel of apples to our cellar store. Mother's delectable apple pies often graced our board at Sunday dinner. Also, a rare treat was when, on a winter evening around the cheery hard-coal heater, Father would suggest, "Obie, why don't you go to the cellar and get us each an apple."

By late winter a malodorous root cellar would prompt Father to assign us the unpleasant task of sorting the potatoes and removing the offensive ones. We would also remove the sprouts from the potatoes yet sound.

Banking our house and insulating the top of our outdoor cistern was another formidable prewinter task. These jobs were always reserved for Saturdays, so that our full work force could be summoned—with no school to interfere.

In preparation, Father would secure a double layer of tar paper over the foundation and completely around the house. Laths tacked to the siding held the tar paper in place. Dirt from the garden was hauled by wheelbarrow and piled against the tar-paper insulating cover to secure it.

Father would arrange for a load of flax straw to be hauled in and spread over and around the cistern top. More dirt was hauled to pile over and hold down this straw covering. The resulting mound, when further buried under ice and snow, became a miniature hill, adapted alike to sledding or a game of king-of-the-hill. With the opportunism of the very young, realization that these tasks had to be reversed in the spring escaped us at the moment. Hauling the dirt back into the garden was not nearly as challenging as the prewinter banking.

Next would come the storm windows. They had to be carried up from the cellar and painstakingly washed. Obie and I would move and steady the ladder as Father mounted it to remove the screens and put on the storm windows. At such times, Obie and I appreciated the merits of a small house.

The observance of Halloween in Hannaford was always a memorable event. The ghosts and goblins of Grandpa's day seemed to take a special delight in overturning outhouses. To thwart or outwit these once-a-year culprits became an almost yearlong obsession with the property owners. Some would bolt the structure to posts imbedded in concrete. Others would resort to a dastardly artifice. On Halloween day, they would move the privy a few feet forward and carefully camouflage the exposed pit with tree branches, corn stalks, or the like. Once victimized by such entrapment, however, the Halloween visitors became wary and carefully probed their approach.

A persistent story had Hank Ferris temporarily imprisoned in his overturned cubicle. He had stationed himself inside to await the coming of expected Halloweeners. Local wags, in relating the tale, insisted that Hank fell asleep and failed to hear the pranksters' approach. Even Hank's imposing bulk was not enough to anchor the little house and over it crashed, doorway down, with a baffled and infuriated Hank within. It took the efforts of half a dozen stalwart men to raise the structure and free Hank. Whether or not this even actually happened, one could readily sympathize with the unwitting victim. The embarrassment of the entrapped man in putting his head through one of the exposed portholes to holler for help must have been insufferable.

Our outhouse had been solidly built by Father himself. Even so, successive upendings had done extensive damage to the roof. Father decided that enough was enough. It was time for drastic action. The sanctity of this family retreat must be safeguarded against further irreparable destruction.

Father had heard that a shotgun shell with rock salt replacing the leaden pellets could become a powerful deterrent to persistent toilet tippers. He became convinced that such a stinging persuader judiciously applied to a retreating rear end would conclusively stop further forays.

Obie was the proud owner of an old shotgun given him by Grandpa Rasmussen. This ancient relic had suffered a burst barrel at the hands of some careless user and the damaged part had been sawed off. This alteration made it a most effective scattergun. Father pressed this unpromising weapon into emergency Halloween service. Almost gleefully he doctored up a couple of shells. Loosening the crimp, he poured out the contained shot. He didn't have any rock salt, but that did not deter him. Father was an inveterate innovator. He decided that ordinary table salt would do quite well.

As soon as darkness fell, Father seated himself in the shadows on our back steps, his secret weapon in readiness. Mother, as a special concession, gave us children permission to stay up later than usual. From the vantage point of a darkened kitchen window, we maintained our expectant vigil. We could distinguish the outline of Father's shadowy bulk on the steps, and out beyond, standing stark and lonely in the pale moonlight, the object of his concern.

The self-appointed guardian of our outhouse did not have too long to wait. We spotted the vague shapes of the nocturnal visitors at about the same time Father did. They materialized out of the dark alley and moved stealthily across the outreach of Mother's garden. Through the open window even the rustling and snapping of crisp corn leaves was clearly audible. We tensed and held our breath, waiting for Father's moment of decision.

We saw him straighten and put the shotgun to his shoulder. Braced for a roaring blast, we heard only a weak "poof." A moment later came the resounding thud and splintering crash of a toppled toilet. Jubilant pranksters beat a noisy and hurried retreat.

We were to learn later the cause for father's failure. The percussion cap of the doctored shell failed to ignite the apparently loosened powder charge. The load of table salt trickled harmlessly out the muzzle.

Father sat alone with his thoughts for what seemed to us a long, long time. Mother was on the verge of urging us to bed with her willow switch when a dour-faced Father made his inglorious entry. He said not a word as he restored Obie's shotgun to its place behind the cellar door. As if in a trance, he marched through the house and up the stairs. We heard his shoes drop with a thump on the bedroom floor above and knew that Father's retreat was complete. He had met the enemy on his own chosen field of battle and had been vanquished. Now he was going to bed. Sympathetic, though slightly bemused, we soon followed.

The following morning saw the usual post-Halloween toilet-raising bee. Neighbors joined forces to get the little houses operational again. The roof of our structure had been nearly broken off, but Father took it philosophically. He discouraged us, however, from disclosing to anyone his abortive fiasco of the preceding night.

Though toppling unoffending outhouses seemed to be the special joy of Halloween pranksters, their nocturnal repertoire was even more inclusive. A tour of Hannaford on the morning after revealed some amazing sights. Frank Olson's dray straddled the ridgepole atop Walt Larson's livery stable. Lizzie Jacobson stared aghast at her beloved horse-drawn buggy perched on the roof of a lumberyard shed. Mr. Wills found two of his cows decked out in horse collars and harness.

The janitor at the school was nearly startled out of his wits in the early morning hours by finding two rampaging goats and a bewildered cow in one of the classrooms. It happened to be the fifth and sixth grade room. The students, including Del and me, received an unexpected forenoon holiday while cleanup operations were under way.

Even the gong above the school doorway, used to summon

lagging scholars from the playground, had been removed and hidden. Until it was retrieved several days later, Mr. Sorenson, our elderly janitor, would appear in the doorway and rather sheepishly ring a little handbell.

First Obie and then Del and I reached Halloweener's estate and were permitted a limited sojourn with other ghosts and goblins. I recall well our first successful onslaught on an outhouse. The structure was solidly set and for a time resisted our stoutest efforts. We had almost despaired of conquering, when it finally began to tilt. With renewed zeal we managed a point of equilibrium where the outhouse teetered precariously for a moment, then yielding to the force of gravity, toppled forward. I can't say that I felt particularly elated, but Del was wildly exultant. To him it was victory of boy and mind over matter—the mastery of a long-admired art.

Heady with this initial success, we prowled the night looking for new worlds to conquer. We were in the vicinity of Walt Larson's livery stable when two shotgun blasts shattered the stillness. In blind panic we took off running, tripping over unseen objects and scrambling up to run again.

Some blocks away we paused in our headlong flight to catch our breath and listen for sounds of fancied pursuit. Each regaled the others with hair-raising accounts of having felt the pattering of buckshot on some part of his body. A missing cap gave credibility to Del's story. He insisted he had heard the zing of the pellet that plucked the cap from his head.

We were all shivering from excitement and fright, and our enthusiasm for further foray had waned considerably. Consensus favored an early departure for the sanctuary of our respective homes.

Mother was more than mildly surprised when we walked in well before her preordained curfew. We did not tell her what had prompted our early return. Mothers seem to get upset about such things.

The next day we retraced our line of flight and found Del's cap caught fast on a low-hanging tree branch. This evidence completely discredited Del's earlier version of what had happened. We now found ourselves entertaining a rather dismaying thought. Perhaps the shots of the previous night were a warning to older and more imminent marauders and not to our innocuous little band at all. In our hearts we much preferred to hear the bullets zing. Del finally gave up trying to find a hole in his cap. Even a tiny one would have been seized upon to salve his wounded vanity.

There were other Halloweens to come, and Del attained stature as an accomplished expert in the now lost art of outhouse tipping. His finest hour came when he engineered the overturning of the massive eight-holer behind the Nordeng & Alm Hotel. That venerable structure had remained unconquerable since its erection in 1900. Del's mathematical mind realized the possibilities of a lever of some kind. A stout oak wagon tongue was dragged in to use as a pry. An unseasonable snow storm masked the covert operation.

The next morning, early-rising hotel guests stared in disbelief as they stepped outside. Their frustration was amplified when a survey of the immediate neighborhood revealed similar despoilment. Emergency crews had to be summoned.

This unhappy morning did little to enhance the already dubious reputation of the Hannaford hostelry. Guests had always dreaded its frigid upstairs rooms on wintry nights. They told of one particular time when a blizzard raged. One by one the chilled guests left their rooms to seek the warmth of the downstairs parlor stove. They spent the remainder of the night clustered around this only source of heat.

The milkman on his early morning round stepped in to warm himself. Icicles from the powdered, driving snow encrusted his eyebrows and moustache. The poor man was half-frozen. One of the sleepy guests had not noticed this newcomer enter. Slack-jawed, he stared in utter disbelief at this icy visage, the fur cap, woolen scarf, upturned collar, mittened hands, and high-buckled overshoes. After a speechless moment he blurted out, "My God, man, which room did you have?"

Halloween seemed to be autumn's last gay fling. Thereafter, each succeeding day became a little colder. The last brown leaf of the poplar came tumbling down and the restless north wind whispered of snowflakes in the offing.

One task remained to make the preparation for winter complete. Father delayed his annual job of butchering a hog until it was quite certain that below-freezing temperatures would prevail. The winter supply of fresh meat was kept frozen outside the house in a large wooden barrel.

Father and a neighbor would join forces on butchering day. Each would procure a sizable hog from an area farmer. The squealing, grunting porkers would be penned in a backyard shed until a suitable day. One essential part of the preparation was to have water boiling in a large metal drum propped over an outdoor fire.

The animal would first be stunned by a heavy blow between the eyes with the blunt heft of a single-bitted axe. A knife thrust into a vulnerable part of the neck would pierce the jugular vein and the hog would quickly bleed to death. The eviscerated carcass was then immersed into the cauldron of boiling water. This scalding process permitted removal of the bristles with a scraping tool. After hanging overnight to cool, the carcass was quartered by laborious hand sawing. The quarters were brought into the house for further cutting up on the kitchen table. Roasts, chops, ribs, and other cuts were individually wrapped in paper obtained at Stub Johnson's meat market and then packed in the freezing barrel. Occasionally one of the thighs of the hog might be taken to Stub Johnson's smokehouse to be cured into ham. This was a somewhat costly luxury, and more often than not the thighs were simply sawed and cut into roasts. A smoke salt was sometimes rubbed into a chunk of the thigh to impart a smoky flavor to the meat. This proved not too satisfactory, and we regarded the pork so treated as a pretty pale substitute for real smoke-cured ham.

Very little of the hog went unused. Portions of the meat of the head and feet were cut up fine, boiled, and pressed into headcheese. Sometimes the blood of the animal was saved and used to make blood pudding or sausage.

An infrequent thawing spell in midwinter would endanger this supply of fresh, frozen meat. I know that Mother and Father were much concerned about this happening, though I don't recall a time that the meat actually spoiled and was lost.

Autumn frosts transformed Bald Hill Creek. The broad valley exchanged its flower-spangled green mantle of summer for bursting milkweed pods and ripe brown cattails. Del and I now walked the banks of the creek to surprise resting ducks among the reeds. We took turns firing Grandpa's old scattergun. If our stalk was successful, one of us would try a potshot with the single-shot .22. Then as the ducks erupted from the water on wildly beating wings, the scattergun would boom. Often the wily birds flew off unscathed. Sometimes we were successful and returned triumphantly with a brace of plump mallards.

We also watched the creek banks for mink sign. Early winter was generally our most successful trapping season. Mink and weasel were our main pursuit. The wary mink were most susceptible to water sets. A stone cairn in the riffles would be baited with part of a rabbit. Traps were placed in the shallow water on the open side of this cache.

Weasels seemed to frequent the rock piles that abounded in

pasture corners and on barren knolls. A similarly baited set was made, except that the traps were covered lightly with grass or leaves. The weasel apparently was not as wary of human scent.

Del and I, or frequently I alone, would check traps before school, often starting out in predawn darkness.

One such morning I was startled to find a live skunk in one of the weasel traps. I dispatched him from a safe distance with the .22. This one had been in a trap before and one foot was missing. An animal caught in a steel trap will often amputate its foot to earn freedom.

For obvious reasons Del and I studiously avoided any entanglement with skunks. It appeared that I was stuck with this one. I was aware that the pelt had a little monetary value and after some mental struggle decided to lug the dead animal home.

Father was still at the breakfast table and even as I closed the door behind me, I saw his nostrils twitch. Then holding his nose, he sputtered, "Phew! Where in the world have you been?"

For several days I was an outcast in my own home and in school. Exaggerated nose-holding gestures greeted me wherever I went. Del used this as another reason to lament his bed partner. "Do I have to sleep with Skunky?"

Sometimes the Bald Hill froze solidly enough for skating before any appreciable amount of snow fell. This would open up still another vista of our beloved creek. Following its meandering course for a mile or two on flashing blades was winter delight without equal.

When we momentarily tired, we would stop and build a fire on the bank. Sometimes we had marshmallows to toast. Often such a stopping point became a sort of base camp. We might pile enough wood on the fire to ensure its burning awhile, leave unnecessary gear to be later retrieved, and continue to skate.

Such were the circumstances on one day in early December. I was the proud possessor of a brand new pair of genuine oiled leather, rawhide-laced, sixteen-inch boots. They reached almost to my kneecaps and my skinny calves made the tops appear loose and ill fitting. No doubt I cut quite a ridiculous figure, but, nonetheless, those boots were my pride and joy.

I had worn them to the creek on this skating trip. My clamp-on skates did not fit well on the thick soles of the new clodhoppers, so I carried an older pair of regular shoes to wear while skating. Consequently my beautiful new boots were among the items left at base camp.

We were rounding the last bend on our return from a sortie up creek when my nose caught an airborne whiff of scorched leather. A gnawing fear lent wings to my skates.

The smouldering remains of my cherished boots lay on a blackened creek bank. Our unguarded campfire had spread to the mat of tinder-dry grass. I carried the charred remnants home—I know not why. Mother, I think, was as grieved as I. Father's shrug seemed to say, "And this is my son?"

9

Mother's Willow Switch

WITH concern for the welfare of four obstreperous boys and finally a baby girl that filled most of her waking hours, Mother's joys, griefs, and fears were her own. Father's inescapable preoccupation was how to provide for his family.

Mother cajoled, kissed, or threatened as circumstances merited. Her great persuader was an often referred to, though seldom used, willow switch. This awesome symbol of authority was kept in plain sight in a corner of the kitchen. Its mere presence acted as a determent to some of our pranks, I'm sure. Now and then, to tease Mother, we would hide the slender whip, but she always seemed to know just where to find it.

Family living in our tiny four-room house necessitated a high degree of accommodation as well as cooperation by all. Meals were prepared and eaten in the kitchen. It seemed that Mother spent most of her waking hours tending kettle or pan atop the coal-burning kitchen range. Water was heated in an attached reservoir and a large oven turned out fragrant, golden loaves of bread. The smells on baking day were impelling enough to make kitchen slaves of Mother's ever-hungry brood. The warm bread or cookies, hot from the pan, had to be sampled.

At mealtime we sat around a sturdy, oilcloth-covered table. Though table prayers were infrequent and brief, we would wait respectfully for Father to start the serving. Then we all fell to with gusto. Table conversation was limited, as we hungrily gobbled our food. It was generally Bumpy who would beguile us with a cheerful recounting of never-ending adventure. Nothing prosaic ever happened to Bumpy. The most humdrum event somehow resolved into exciting fantasy.

After baby sister Tina assumed a high chair position at the

table, she competed with Bumpy for attention. Father always drank his hot coffee from the saucer, and his noisy inhalations would evoke ecstatic response from Tina. I'm not certain Father shared in the general hilarity that invaribably followed.

We always had enough to eat, though I'm certain that it taxed all of Mother's ingenuity to plan meals on her severely stringent budget. Bread, boiled potatoes, either fresh or canned garden vegetables, soup, oatmeal, and pancakes were staples. Mainly for Father's sake, meat had to be included occasionally, generally with the evening meal. It was mostly pork—salted or canned pork in the warmer months and fresh, frozen side pork during the winter. Fresh fish from the Bald Hill Creek provided a welcome change during the spring and summer months. An occasional wild duck and cottontail rabbits were relished during the fall and winter.

We learned not to waste food and were chided if an uneaten portion was left on our plates. I don't think we were fussy eaters, with one notable exception. For some unexplained reason, none of us children shared Father's and Mother's taste for onions. The sight of five youngsters carefully picking bits or even the whole offending bulb from Mother's tasty dishes was viewed with some displeasure by both of our parents.

Once when Grandpa Rasmussen was a dinner guest, he spotted Obie removing the small whole onions from his soup. Though Grandpa was quite aware of our dislike of onions, he innocently inquired, "What are you doing, Obie?"

"I don't like onions, Grampaw!"

"But, Obie, those aren't onions—they are 'loi.' "

Obie gave Grandpa a quizzical look, but out of deference he gingerly tasted one of Grandpa's loi. He grimaced and after a moment's solemn meditation ventured apologetically, "But Grampaw, loi sure taste like onions, don't they?"

For a moment Father almost strangled on a mouthful of soup, which only added to Grandpa Rasmussen's discomfiture.

Like all youngsters, we went through the cookie jar raiding stage. At a quite tender age we learned that we couldn't have everything we wanted all of the time. The reprimand was sometimes reinforced with the ever-handy willow wand. We had to be content with what was given us or with what we could snitch. Del and I once returned in late afternoon from an outing along the Bald Hill. We were famished, and Mother happened to be gone. A platterful of cold meatloaf stored on a pantry shelf was forthwith discovered. Del and I retired with this enticing find to the back step, where we proceeded to wolf it down to the last morsel. Our well-filled tummies gave way to aching hearts when a tearful Mother informed us that we had eaten what was meant to be supper for all.

A washstand and cistern pump occupied a corner of the kitchen. There was also a place for water pail and dipper. Drinking water was carried from neighbor Jackson's well. Under the established division of labor in our household, the older boys were to fetch the water. That narrowed the task pretty much to Obie and me. Del would walk around with his tongue hanging out from thirst before he would grudgingly pick up the empty pail. Obie and I would often pretend not to hear the clink of the dipper in the bottom as Del tried to assuage his thirst by extracting the last drop. Each would try to outwait the other, until Mother would end the war of attrition by sending one of us hustling out the door, pail in hand.

On bitterly cold winter mornings, firstcomers to the pump might find it frozen. This necessitated a teakettle of boiling water to thaw it out. We were struggling with this task one morning when Del prevailed upon me to touch the tip of my tongue to the iron pump handle. Though the backward jerk of my head was almost instantaneous, skin from the forward portion of my tongue was ripped away—frozen fast to the unyielding iron. The pain from the raw and bleeding tongue sent me home screaming. A distraught Mother wielded her willow switch heartily on Del's bottom. Father had far less sympathy. In his words, "How could a kid be so dumb?"

A row of hooks behind the kitchen door and another in the entryway to our combined coal and root cellar were intended for jackets, caps, and coats. Under Mother's watchful eye, they were used. A coat and cap slung over a convenient chair or carelessly tossed in a corner were quickly identified with their negligent owner. Overshoes were lined up near the door, and we were constantly admonished to wipe our feet. Mud and snow were tracked in nonetheless, and Mother did a lot of mopping up on her linoleum-covered floors. During the winter months she also had to contend with wet mittens drying either atop the stove or on the opened oven door.

On washday a goodly part of Mother's kitchen became laundry room. A washtub and stand and a copper boiler were lugged up from their storage place along the cellar stairway. Water was heated in the boiler on the kitchen range. All clothes were rubbed and scrubbed by hand on a washboard. Mother did enjoy the luxury of a hand-turned clothes ringer that clamped to the side of her washtub. Clothes were hung outside to dry. In wintertime they would freeze stiff on the line. The long-handled underwear, ranging downward in size from Father's 44 to Bumpsy's diminutive proportions, assumed grotesque shapes. Undue bending in this frozen state could damage the fabric, so they were wrestled indoors like headless ghosts. A few minutes in the warm air of the kitchen would collapse them enough so that they could be draped over a clothes rack to complete their drying.

It was little wonder that Mother's hands remained red, swollen, cracked, and sore much of the time. The strong lye soap required to get grimy work clothes respectably clean was no respecter of women's hands.

The rite of the Saturday night bath was likewise performed in the kitchen. One at a time, starting with the youngest, we clambered into Mother's washtub. Again water had to be heated. All waste water had to be carried outside and dumped in a sinkhole off to one side of the garden. This in itself was heavy, never-ending drudgery, and though Obie and I struggled manfully with the task, Mother often had to give us a hand.

After the supper dishes were cleared and washed, the kitchen table became our school homework desk. Many indeed were the arithmetic problems I struggled with mightily. My teacher must have loved long division. It seemed to me, at least, that we would never get beyond that part of our book. "Do the next twenty problems." It was like a stuck phonograph needle. If the answer came out even, it wasn't so bad, but boy, those that had remainders! Many was the night that I was the last one sitting at the table. Obie was a whiz at arithemtic and Del also breezed through his problems with little trouble. They would finish all their written assignments long before I did and would sprawl on the floor alongside the parlor heater and either read a story or play some game. Often Mother would leave her mending or ironing and come to my rescue, helping me through the remaining problems. Tears of frustration were often in my eyes, but Mother was always kind and patient. If she was tired and worn, she never let on.

A rotund hard-coal heater took up considerable space in our parlor. We never tired of admiring the distorted, grimacing images of our faces reflected in its highly polished, nickel-plated accouterments. The smoothly rounded surfaces were wonderful to warm cold hands or feet against. In wintertime, we both dressed and undressed within its circle of pleasant warmth. The cheerful glow of the fire within shone through isinglass doors and half lit the room. Mother often popped corn by opening one of these doors. A long wooden handle permitted the wire popper to be held and shaken close to the intense heat.

Two large oak rocking chairs and what we called a library table also graced our parlor. Father usually occupied one of these rockers.

He would often fall asleep reading. The bows of his store-bought reading glasses were too short to properly extend over his ears and the gentle movement of his breathing as he dozed would eventually dislodge them from their perch on his nose. Father would come to with a start, retrieve and readjust the spectacles, read a few more lines, and then give a repeat performance. It was a rare moment when Mother could enjoy the other rocker. Even as she sat, there was usually mending in her lap. If not that, we were clustered around her chair while she read to us. The only newspaper that arrived in our home with regularity was a Scandinavian weekly called *Decorah Posten*. A regular feature was a story published in serial form. Mother would read and translate to us simultaneously. In the same manner we laughed at the antics of Ola and Per in the weekly comic strip. We waited with impatience the scheduled arrival of this weekly paper. It seemed that each installment always ended in the most exciting place.

An abrupt stairway along one wall of the parlor led to the two upstairs bedrooms. My three brothers and I shared one of these tiny rooms under the roof slope. The ceiling slanted toward the eaves and only Bumpy could move along the outer edge of the beds without bending. Obie and Bumpy shared one of the double beds, Del and I the other. Perhaps five feet of space separated the two beds. A small clothes closet was ample for our meager wardrobes and afforded Mother a little storage space besides. A chamber pot stood in the hallway between the two bedrooms. This was a highly regarded convenience, especially on cold winter nights and mornings when we all avoided the unpleasant sojourn to the outhouse. Emptying this ofttimes brimming receptacle was but one more of Mother's labors of love. The bedrooms were often suffocatingly hot in the summer and frigid in winter. A heavy patchwork quilt, the top made of sewn-together squares of worsted suiting over a wool batting, covered each bed. Even with the warmth such a quilt afforded, Mother would see fit on the coldest nights to bury Del and me further under a huge horsehide coat.

For a few years I was an occasional bedwetter. This would infuriate Del, and he loudly lamented each time that I had elected to do the wetting either in the middle of the bed or on his side. Mother assured him that this was not by design, but because the bed sagged in the middle. I'm sure that to this day, Del remains unconvinced.

Contrary to what Del thought, my chagrin and shame over these infrequent incidents are painful memories.

Bedbugs abounded in spite of Mother's unending war against them. At least once a month she would spray kerosene behind moldings, into all cracks and crevices, over the bed frames and springs, and even on the corners of the mattresses. These pests were nigh impossible to exterminate. Often as we lay in bed we would spot them crawling up the wall or ceiling. Bumpy had no qualms about impaling them on the end of a pin or needle and then dropping them into the chamber pot to swim or drown.

One winter one of us managed to bring home the itch (scabies) and promptly infected all except Mother, Father, and Tina. We scratched until the skin was raw, often crying in misery from the affliction. Doc Benson, Hannaford's general practitioner who treated both man and beast, mixed up a sulphur ointment which Mother used to alleviate our torment. It seemed to be effective, because in due time the irritation left and we were our normal squirming selves again.

Sniffles and colds were accepted as a part of winter. They seemed to be with us constantly from about Christmastime through late spring. The term "snot-nosed kid" was unmistakably no misnomer. Busy boys found it handy and convenient to wipe the offending proboscis on the sleeve of jacket or blouse. Mother frowned on such practice as being both unsanitary and unsightly. "Blow your nose" was a repetitious admonition from Father and Mother alike.

A chest cold was taken quite seriously, as it might turn into dreaded pneumonia. Mother put a lot of faith in the efficacy of a musterole chest rub. The stuff didn't smell so good, and we also disliked the scratchy woolen cloth that had to enfold neck and chest. A mustard plaster applied to the afflicted parts was even more distasteful. The tiny sip of chokecherry wine that topped off the treatment was meager compensation for the unpleasant preliminaries.

No matter how hectic the day, Mother somehow managed to keep her equanimity. Friends and neighbors found her able to relax over an afternoon cup of coffee. She was resolutely selective, however, in her involvement in activities outside her home. If there were daily tasks that needed her attention, and it was only infrequently that there weren't, no enticement could swerve her from the appointed duty. A gregarious neighbor, Mrs. Lund, aften attempted to inveigle Mother into accompanying her to afternoon Ladies Aid gatherings. Even Mrs. Lund's strongest plea, "Just think of all the good things there'll be to eat," did not often change Mother's mind.

I know Father loved and certainly deserved a little snooze when opportunity afforded. Mother was adamant in her refusal to nap at any time. In midafternoon, if she felt sleepy, she would pause in her household routine and go outside to work in her garden or flower beds.

Mother's life with Father was generally tranquil. Father worked hard to provide for·us, and I know he loved his family. His only indulgence was his Saturday night trek to the local pool hall for a rather harmless game of rummy with cronies. On occasion, Father might sit in on a poker game, but he knew his limitations, and money he could ill afford to gamble was one.

Mother had an unyielding aversion to strong drink, and Father wisely respected her judgment. One unfortunate exception left an indelible impression on my mind. On this fateful night I happened to be the only one of the children sleeping at home. Tina was spending the night next door at her close friend Janie's home. Bumpy had accompanied his friends, the Willses, to the county seat that day to take in the annual fair and by prearrangment was to spend the night at their home. Obie and Del were spending a few days at an uncle's farm.

It must have been nearly midnight when I was startled into wakefulness by the unnatural sound of my parents' voices raised in angry discussion. They were quarreling down in the kitchen. Father had been drinking and came home tipsy. With the thought of frightening him into sobriety, Mother foolishly threatened him with an old, useless pistol that one of us had salvaged from a junk pile.

An enraged Father would not be bluffed, and Mother was forced to retreat in utter panic up the stairs. Her scream for help rang in my ears, and I heard their feet pounding up the steps. My eye fell upon a heavy stone Indian hammer that we used for a bedroom doorstop. Instinctively I seized it and with this formidable weapon bearded Father at the top of the stairs. Mother had managed to dart by me into the bedroom.

Taken aback by my sudden appearance, Father stopped his upward charge. His wild eyes appraised the upraised rock. "Don't come any farther, Father! Please, Father, don't make me hurt you."

My white, stricken face, more than the terrified warning, shocked Father into reality. He stared at me in wondering disbelief for what seemed to me an eternity. Then in stunned bewilderment he turned and stumbled down the staircase.

We heard him leave the house, and a frightened boy and his mother broke into uncontrollable sobbing. Father returned shortly with Jack Rierson, Hannaford's town constable.

An almost incoherent Father repeated his charges: "She was going to shoot me," and with a trembling finger in my direction, "he was going to take me with a rock."

Between sobs, I blurted out what I knew of the unhappy event. The constable's keen eye sized up the rusted pistol with its missing cylinder. It was scarcely a lethal weapon. He wisely took Father's arm and urged him to spend the night with him at his home. Father by now was quite agreeable, and Mr. Rierson bid Mother and me a kindly "good-night."

Next morning the three of us, Mother, Father, and I, ate our breakfast in foreboding silence. I know that we were all completely miserable and penitent. It was only after Father downed his last saucer of coffee that he spoke. His voice was low and disconsolate. "Harvey, you will have to leave this house."

I was aware of Mother's involuntary gasp. Momentarily my world stopped.

Father pushed back his chair and started to rise. Instead, he leaned forward and bowed his head. Then we heard him cry out in anguish, "Lord, forgive us for what we have done."

From the bottom of our hearts, Mother and I breathed a fervent, "Amen."

Before another day dawned, amicable relations had been restored. With the Lord's help, forgiveness among us was complete. The terror of that one dark night faded and was replaced by a new serenity. No more was said about my leaving, and I believe Father and I experienced an even deeper kinship. To the best of my knowledge, this was Father and Mother's first and last violent quarrel.

They did not always see eye to eye, of course, on all matters. One such divergent view and its ultimate resolvement had a profound effect on the future of my brothers and me. If Father's view had prevailed, our formal schooling would have ended upon completion of the eighth grade. His own education had ended in grade six when he was put to work full time on the farm. Father saw little use in a boy going to high school when he could be starting to make his own way in the world.

Here, however, Mother firmly put her foot down. Mother had completed the eighth grade and once had dreamed of becoming a teacher. Those dreams had been cut short by the untimely death of her mother. Mother was determined that her sons would receive high school education. In this resolution Mother's judgment gained Father's grudging acceptance.

Mother, indeed, fulfilled many roles. Throughout those boyhood years on the Bald Hill, Mother's love and concern for her children was constant. It has remained so these many years.

One of my happiest memories is that of hearing her call for us to come home as darkness fell at the end of a long summer day. Often we were playing a block away in Bill Lund's yard. We would first hear her summons from where she stood in our own front yard, "Obie! Obie! Harvey! Del! Bumpy! Come home now. It's bedtime."

If we were tardy in heeding her first bidding, one of us would soon spot her familiar figure approaching out of the dusk. As she would emerge into the light of the corner street lamp, we could also see the good old willow switch in her hand.

That was all the urging we needed. We loved to beat Mother home by scurrying across a neighbor's backyard, out of her sight behind his house. By the time Mother had made her leisurely way back along the sidewalk, we were nonchalantly starting to undress. Out of the corner of an eye, we would smugly watch as she restored the willow switch to its corner station. Mother, I'm sure, was perfectly content to permit this roguish bit of byplay. Her children were home and safe.

10

Singing Wires

EVEN Samuel Morse as he tapped out his famous message, "What hath God wrought," could not have been as thrilled as I was when the sounder of my homemade receiving set began to click. My pal, Millard, was on the key in his house almost a full block away. Two strands of much-spliced copper wire tacked to electric light poles carried his stuttering dots and dashes. Dot dot dot dot, four dots, followed by a lengthy pause. Translating from my hand-printed copy of the Morse code I penciled the letter H on my tablet. Next a single dot meant E. Again the pause and then a single dash for the letter L. The word, HELLO, took shape and then HARVEY. Then the wire went dead, and it was my turn.

Millard had received his telegraph set for Christmas. The brass sounder and key were mounted together on a wood base. When hooked up to a dry cell battery, a touch on the key would produce a sharp clicking sound from the anvil on the sounder. It was a fascinating instrument and we soon realized its possibilities. If only we had another telegraph set! Buying one was out of the question, so I proceeded to make one. Necessary materials were scrounged from junk piles behind the town's garage and also from the telephone office. A flat piece of wood, a T-shaped piece of iron, some iron nails, a flexible strip of brass, some brass screws, and some insulated wire were assembled. The finished instrument bore but remote resemblance to Millard's polished equipment, but it worked.

Finding enough copper wire to string our line was more of a problem. We had to span a distance of about 400 feet. At first we tried a single wire and ground, but our source of power, a half-dozen dry cells hooked in series, proved too weak. Finally we managed the second strand of wire, and communications were opened. Father

92

was startled half out of his wits one morning when the machine began to click just as he was pulling on his trousers. In the one-legged dance that ensued, his backside made contact with a hot portion of the hard-coal heater. We heard his howl of anguish clear upstairs. What Harvey had wrought didn't exactly impress him at the moment.

At about the time Millard and I were tapping out our Morse messages, the first radio receiving sets were appearing in Hannaford. An outside aerial running from a pole high on the housetop to a corresponding pole on shed or barn roof was visible evidence of a radio within. Ole Thorseth's father owned the town's only hardware store and thereby became the envied possessor of the town's first radio. Ole boastfully informed us that it was a seven-tube super heterodyne. It boasted a separate horn-type loudspeaker and three dials, which had to be manipulated to bring a station in. For several months Ole could command an audience at will. We would listen spellbound as he regaled us with his secondhand accounts of the previous night's listening. Ole logged the stations that his father pulled in: KDKA in Pittsburgh, WWJ in Detroit, KMOX in St. Louis, WHO in Des Moines—strange, faraway places with their mysterious call letters.

Our own first radio receiving set was a two-tube Crosley purchased in October 1924. With batteries and outside aerial the total cost was about forty dollars. Obie used most of his summer wages to buy it. Father wasn't much in favor of the idea, but on this occasion he was outvoted. The battery-powered set was equipped with two sets of earphones. It was possible for four persons to listen at once by separating each pair of earphones. We even devised a loudspeaker of sorts by placing the earphones face down on the bottom of an inverted metal dishpan. As many as six or eight people might crowd in circular fashion around this amplifier, with head inclined inward and ear cocked for the all too faint sound.

Father's initial resistance was soon overcome and he became an avid listener. His disappointment was keen when neighbors dropped in to hear the radio and it emitted nothing but squeals and squawks. "You should'a been here las' night," Father would lament sadly.

The advent of radio into our home kind of outmoded our telegraphic effort. To keep abreast, Millard and I experimented with wireless. Induction coils out of a Model T Ford were ingeniously hooked in to give our battery current a higher potential. We endeavored to send Morse code signals out over the air by hooking our sending key to the radio aerial and ground. We succeeded in disrupting evening radio reception in our neighborhood. When irate listeners traced the source of the interference, our wireless transmissions were summarily banned.

Partly because early radio reception was quite unpredictable, we did not become addicted to listening. We could take or leave the antics of The Happiness Boys or the music of Chubby Parker and his five-string banjo. Always outdoor pursuits beckoned—even in the dead of winter. School homework took precedence, but there were those rare times when none had been assigned. Friday and Saturday evenings were the schoolboy's special delight.

Sledding on moonlit nights was a favorite winter pastime. The road leading eastward out of Hannaford descended into and across the Bald Hill valley. Horse-drawn sleighs packed the road surface on this hill to an icy smoothness ideal for the narrow steel runners of our American Flyer sleds. A running start and a belly flop onto the skimming sled assured a speedy coast of upwards of an eighth of a mile or farther. The sled was only slowed to a stop when it reached the incline on the far side of the valley. We vied mightily for the farthest ride. It quickly dawned on us that even a little extra weight made a difference and that the heavier rider had an advantage. A speedier take off helped even the odds. The hiss of the runners underneath and the rush of frosty air against tingling nose and cheeks were heady wine to the sledders. Occasional sparks, as steel runner struck exposed pebbles, were as twinkling fireflies down the length of the slope.

A main road leading west out of town passed our house and added yet another dimension to our winter sledding. Snow-choked roads became impassable for winter auto travel and the family jitney was generally put up on blocks for the winter. Farm folk came to town in droves on Saturdays in all modes of horsedrawn sleighs: bobsleds, covered rigs, and cutters. In late afternoon the homeward-bound procession began. An eager gang of boys were usually waiting with their sleds. A long single rope was attached to each sled. Running alongside a moving sleigh, the ride hooker would pull the free end of the rope through the opening of a brace iron and dropping back mount the bouncing little sled. It was a tricky maneuver and sometimes boy and sled went rolling. The eager horses, sensing a warm barn and fragrant hay at journey's end, needed no urging to break into a spanking trot.

Following a successful hookup, the jubilant passenger would ride as far into the countryside as fancy dictated. Always we were mindful of the walk back pulling the empty sled and would reluctantly disengage after a thrilling ride of upward of a half mile. Del had a preference for shorter and more frequent rides and was usually the first to unhook. The skimming rider would terminate the excursion by loosening his grip on the end of the rope and letting it slip free. Once a knot I had fashioned to halt raveling became wedged in an angle iron brace and I found myself an unwilling prisoner aboard my bounding sled. I was bound fast to a covered rig and the driver was unaware of his uninvited passenger. Apparently he could not hear my cries for help and I was being carried well beyond our usual disembarkation point. Descending darkness on that brief December day added to my concern. How far the rig might travel I had no idea. Finally, in desperation, I rolled from my speeding sled. By the time I got to my feet the rig, with captive sled, was perhaps a hundred feet up the road—and moving. I took off in running pursuit, gasping a little prayer that the horses might slow to a walk. Miraculously they did, on a slight hill. Just when it seemed that I could run no farther, I caught up and with a final stumbling effort freed the rope.

The horses resumed their trot at the top of the incline and I watched the rig disappear into the dusk. I had my precious sled, and that was all that mattered. With thankful heart I started the long trek back toward town. The others were gathered at the supper table when I made my abashed entrance. To head off embarrassing questions, I blurted out with all the enthusiasm a tired boy could muster, "Boy, did I have a dandy ride!"

"How far d'ja go?" queried Del.

"Way past the Langdon Bridge," I replied, "and was it ever fun!"

Incredulous and slack jawed, Del for a moment stared at me and slowly shook his head. He mumbled something under his breath and almost strangled on his next huge mouthful of food. I embellished no further, but fell to my supper with gusto. My fiasco had assumed the outward trappings of a triumph. I decided to let well enough alone. My account was close enough to the truth that I could live with my conscience.

Winter blizzards piled our snowfall into huge and often grotesque drifts. At times the snow was almost treetop level around Mr. Wigen's garden and yard. It was there that the neighborhood youngsters gathered to tunnel a labyrinth of snow caves and to play king-of-the-hill. Mr. Wigen must have wondered why he was so singularly blessed with the presence of neighborhood urchins winter and summer alike. The attraction of his strawberry patch I'm sure he could understand, but after all—there were other snowbanks.

Mr. Wigen must have been a patient man. Most of us who

Aunt Christie at her telephone switchboard, 1910. It was part of her job to cheerfully dispense correct time, weather reports, and local news.

Sledding was our favorite winter pastime.

The heated family cutter provided a snug trip to town or to visit neighbors.

Horses drew all the winter sleighs whether they were bobsleds, covered rigs, or cutters.

romped on his delightful snowbanks did feel a mite sorry for him when we heard that he was laid up with a sprained back. Mrs. Wigen confided to Mrs. Lund what had happened. Sympathetic Mrs. Lund passed the story on. "Why the poor man, he was on his way through the trees to empty the bucket from his water closet when he broke through the roof of a snow tunnel. He dropped four or five feet and got stuck with only his head showing. He got sloshed all over when the bucket spilled on top of him. The poor man could have froze to death out there if Mr. Wills hadn't been passing by and heard him holler."

A January thaw, or later the softening breezes of spring, was conducive to snowballing. Obie and Ole might hole up in their exclusive fortress and bombard us lesser fry long range. "Take cover," Del would screech, and a mad scramble would ensue. Tumbling one atop the other we would dive for the protective cover of our own stronghold. A strategy session was in order. Obie and Ole had the better throwing arms, but we had the advantage of numbers. Stockpiling snowballs was our first concern. Then with each little trooper carrying as many snowballs as his size permitted, we would deploy our forces on four sides of our entrenched enemy. Upon the agreed signal, a war whoop by Del or Bumpy, we would storm the citadel. The beleaguered Obie and Ole would score hits on some of the attackers but usually wound up taking a punishing close-in pelting.

Sometimes innocent passersby became the targets for either errant or sometimes intentionally aimed snowballs. Some of these unwilling victims did not take kindly to the pastime and would give determined chase after the offender. If caught, the culprit might suffer the indignity of having his face vigorously washed with snow.

The unmarried teachers had a boardinghouse close to where we lived. They usually walked as a group for their noon luncheon. Their customary path took them up an alley only half a block from our backyard and then behind neighbor Jackson's two-story house. One prime snowballing day a daring plan formed in my mind. I hurried home from school upon noon dismissal and fashioned half a dozen firm snowballs. I loitered nonchalantly in the yard until the unsuspecting teachers passed out of sight behind the intervening house. In rapid-fire succession I lofted the snowballs up and over the roof, leading each one several feet ahead of the preceding one. Then I dashed into our house and peeked out of a window. As the mystified teachers emerged into view they turned and gawked in the direction of our yard. I could only conclude that my missiles must have at least landed close.

I repeated this performance once too often. The teachers proved more observant than I reckoned. They associated my loitering in the yard with the bombardment out of the sky and informed Father. When they told of the snowballs coming at them over the top of Jackson's imposing house, Father was incredulous. When he asked me about it point-blank I had to confess. A stern admonishment by Father put an end to this particular harassment of my esteemed mentors. I had expected to fare worse, but I think that the feat had impressed Father. "With that kind of throwing arm, maybe the kid will grow up to be a baseball player."

During the early 1920s an almost annual midwinter event in Hannaford was the appearance of a Greek strongman, Nikolaos Khrisoupolis, and his trained wrestling bear. Bumpy was always the first to spot the advance poster bearing an impressive picture of "Nick, the Greek and His Wrestling Bear." For most of the week preceding his usual one-night stand the boys of Hannaford could think and talk of little else. Would Nick or the huge black bear come out on top in their epic struggle?

The show was invariably staged on a Friday or Saturday night. A vacant store building served as a hall for such performances. The up-front seats for the small fry were merely planks supported by nail kegs. We thought nothing of standing in the winter cold for an hour in order to be first in line for tickets and a ringside seat.

The big moment finally arrived. The strongman would slowly remove his robe. He was built on the order of a gorilla—short, almost squat, and barrel-chested, with bulging biceps and powerful, bandy legs. His swarthy skin and dark curly hair were strangely alien in the predominantly Scandinavian community. We were treated first to a flexing of those mighty muscles—front, side, and back. The rippling ropes of muscle on that dark, glistening body brought muffled "oohs" and "ahs" from the front-row nail-keggers. Next would come prodigious feats of weight lifting. Heavy barbell weights were added one by one until they seemed impossible for even the mighty Nick to budge. Collectively we would grunt and strain in sympathy with the superhuman effort being exerted. Up, up, up—inches at a time—beads of sweat popping out on that distorted, grimacing visage—almost—there! His arms were now completely extended. An audible sigh of relief would go up as the formidable barbell was lowered to the canvas.

And now the moment we had been waiting for. The trained bear would be led out and introduced. In his halting, broken English

Nikolaos would tell us that her name was Trikkala. There was a brass-studded collar around Trikkala's neck and she was on a stout leash. We were grateful for the leash and got some comfort from Nikolaos's powerful restraining arm upon it. During those first uneasy moments I, for one, would have gladly relinquished my front row seat for a more sheltered spot in the hall. Trepidation soon yielded to amusement when Trikkala became the clown. Upon urging from Nikolaos the bear reared erect and performed an amusing dance shuffle. Our laughter and applause quickened when Trikkala stood on her head. She concluded each antic by sitting down on her haunches and begging for food with her forepaws stretched out. Her reward was a tidbit snuffled from her master's hand.

We were quite enchanted with Trikkala and eager for the much-heralded wrestling match. We shivered in anticipation. Trikkala would be muzzled for this part of the act. She submitted to this indignity with her first sign of irritation—some low, throaty growling.

Prodded by her adversary, the bear reared to full height. The huge animal seemed to dwarf Nikolaos. Because of her long, coarse hair and loose skin she no doubt looked bigger than she was. Father told us later that this bear weighed somewhat over 300 pounds—about average for a black bear. Nikolaos at 240 pounds was outweighed by at least 60 pounds.

Nikolaos warily circled the bear, tantalizing the shuffling, growling animal by dancing in and out. Always he sought to keep out of reach of those short, powerful forepaws. Approaching from back or side he would try to knock the lumbering Trikkala off balance by butting her with a muscular shoulder. Each time, the short-tempered animal responded with a ferocious, spine-tingling roar of unbridled rage and a redoubled effort to reach her tormentor. At times they clinched and rolled, and in the roaring melee we feared for Nikolaos. Each time he miraculously broke free, but not without tremendous exertion. Angry red welts across the Greek's back and chest were visible evidence of the punishment he took. The wrestling match would end in an apparent draw with neither man or beast able to overcome.

Removal of the muzzle seemed to mollify Trikkala's rage. Rewarded with another tidibt she was soon the docile clown again.

By the second or third billing, a bit of novelty must have worn off. The act held sustained appeal for the younger audiences, but waning adult interest led showman Nikolaos to add a new wrinkle.

The advance poster proclaimed a fifty dollar payoff to the wrestler who could best Nick the Greek in a two-out-of-three-fall match.

Jack Rierson, one of our heroes on the Hannaford baseball team, had also gained local renown as a wrestler. It didn't require too much urging by Jack's friends to get him to accept the challenge.

The two men presented quite a contrast as they shook hands in the center of the improvised ring. Jack stood a head taller than the Greek and was lithe and strong. Nikolaos carried a forty-pound weight advantage, however, and his pillarlike legs made Jack's look like toothpicks.

The match was to be catch-as-catch-can, two out of three falls, or until one of the wrestlers should yield. For better or for worse, Stub Skow was pressed into service as the referee. Loyalties now were all with Jack, and the spectators hollered their lusty encouragement. Spirits sagged when the Greek strongman scored the first fall. They rose again when Jack came close to pinning Nikolaos in the second go. A groan of disappointment arose when the slippery Greek broke Jack's hold and wriggled free. The end came with stunning finality. Nikolaos locked those powerful bandy legs around Jack's midsection in a crushing scissors hold. A gasping Jack managed to signal referee Stub that he had had enough.

There was no joy in Hannaford that night. Our idol had been toppled by the Greek strongman. Though bent, our spirits were not broken. We still had boundless faith in Jack and vowed there would be a day of reckoning.

The wild clangor of the fire bell was a fearsome sound at any time, but was especially terrifying in the dead of a cold winter night. One such night of terror and temptation remains etched in my mind. The dread peal awakened us shortly after midnight. Father hurriedly donned his clothes and took off on a run. Shortly a red glow lit the sky over the downtown area, and we knew that it was a major fire. Obie, Del, and I prevailed upon Mother to let us get dressed and go to watch. She was willing to accompany us.

The fire had started in a pool hall and by the time we arrived was threatening adjoining buildings. One of the endangered structures housed the Thorseth Hardware Store and a host of volunteers were carrying out and piling the store's contents in the street. We stood but a short distance from a jumbled pile of rescued merchandise. Atop one stack stood a familiar cardboard display holder. It held the very harmonicas I had been admiring ever since the Christmas stock had appeared a week or two earlier. They were priced at ninety-nine cents, which was quite a lot of money to save. I had about given up the thought of owning one.

Now here they were, only a few feet from me! I could only think that providence had placed them there within my grasp. They might well have all been destroyed in the raging fire. Surely one would not be missed. In the bustle and excitement it would be easy to slip one in my pocket. Spectators, including Mother, were intent on the leaping flames. No one would see me. Never had I been so sorely tempted!

Then my darting eyes fell upon Mr. Thorseth. The unhappy man, head sunk forward into the upturned collar of his overcoat, stood and watched the raging inferno destroy his business. In that moment he looked so old, so frail, so thoroughly beaten. In the dancing light I saw a tear glisten as it coursed down his furrowed cheek. My own eyes were blurred as I deliberately moved farther into the background. A tinge of sadness and a blush of shame overcame me. How thankful I was that the coveted mouth organ was not in my pocket. Before the fire was controlled, several buildings had been destroyed. The bank on the corner was spared, protected by its stone-wall construction. The burned out space left an unsightly gap on Hannaford's main street. Mr. Thorseth suffered severe depression after the loss of his store and never did completely recover.

My desire for a harmonica proved to be but a fleeting fancy. I settled for a Jew's harp. For days on end I practiced "Yankee Doodle" and "Oh, Susanah." The monotonous twanging annoyed everyone but found particular disfavor with Father. I got the message when he suggested that I practice in the outhouse.

Hannaford's most impressive business establishment was The Mercantile Store. We loved to browse its many aisles on busy Saturday evenings while Mother did her weekly shopping. The store had four ill-defined areas: women's apparel, bolts of cloth, countless spools of thread, skeins of wool yarn, and other such sundries occupied several aisles on one side of the store; boys' and gents' furnishings had the center aisles; and hardware items and furniture were on the far side. There, kegs of nails, coils of rope, linoleum rugs, stacks of paint cans, baby carriages, bamboo fishing poles, and horse collars hung on pegs combined to make a delightful maze for games of tag or hide-and-seek. Mr. Lund, owner of the Mercantile, and clerks alike were tolerant to a point with the shenanigans of the young, nonpaying customers. After that point it was "Out!"

Mr. Lund and his bookkeeper presided over the store's open office area which occupied space almost in the center of the store. They worked within the confines of a high circular counter, its access limited to a formidable swinging door. There were perhaps a half-dozen regular clerks to wait on the customers. All sales slips and money payments were sped to this central bookkeeping on a network of overhead cables stretching from each department in the store. The salesclerk would place slip and money in a small metal box and a downward pull on an attached rope handle would send this little aerial trolley skimming up a slightly inclined wire to the cashier. Sometimes the clerk's tug on the starting rope was not sufficiently strong to propel the money-box carrier to its destination. It might stall midway and roll back down to its starting point. The second impetus was usually sufficient. Change was returned to the waiting clerk by the same overhead route, this time on a slightly downward course with gravity alone supplying momentum. Occasionally a congenial clerk would permit a youngster to give the starting pull. It certainly gave the favored one a feeling of importance, especially if the tiny tramcar made it to the cashier's cage on the first attempt.

A grocery counter occupied the rear of the store. Here the aroma of freshly ground coffee mingled with the pungent odor of pickled herring and the tang of smoked meats and fish. On a shelf in back of the counter stood stone crocks of homemade butter bought or bartered from local farmwives. A wooden toothpick was used by the prospective buyer to sample these wares. Mother knew full well that the butter varied greatly in quality. Often the supplier's name sufficed to assure a sale. The butter from some farms was uniformly good. Butter from other crocks the clerk would not even offer for sampling. As one confided to Mother, "That butter is fit only for axle grease."

Many food items were sold from bulk stock and the purchase weighed on a large counter scale. In the case of coffee the measured amount of coffee beans would be dumped into the hopper of a ponderous, hand-turned grinder. It was indeed a happy moment for me if I was permitted to turn the heavy fly-wheel crank.

Clothing items at the Mercantile were generally priced somewhat higher than comparable items in the mail-order catalogs. There were a few exceptions, and our fleece-lined leather mittens with their elasticized wristlets were usually bought at the Mercantile. Once a special bargain was offered on some surplus U.S. Marine dress jackets. Del and I greatly admired the flannelette navy blue cloth and the red piping on cuffs, pockets, and collar. The style was World War I vintage, with a short, stand-up collar which clasped tightly around the neck. The buttoned-down shoulder flaps for over-the-shoulder harness did not escape our attention. Our pleading finally overcame Mother's objections. Even the smallest size was ill fitting, and I'm sure that Del and I cut ridiculous figures in the oversized jackets. We discovered to our dismay that the military-cut collars gave little protection to the neck on cold winter days. The collars chafed and the exposed neck area became red and chapped. Mother loved us far too much to say, "I told you so."

Hannaford's Commercial Club put on an annual Father and Sons Banquet. Father was not a member of the club, and he had four sons. Some members of the club were not fathers or had sons who were grown. Mr. Otterson, the druggist, was in this latter category and asked me to be his son for the evening.

Mother made certain that I was well scrubbed and that my shoes were shined. Father tied one of his neckties for me and both he and Mother appeared mighty proud. The thought came to me, "If Father did belong to the Commercial Club, which son would he take to the banquet? Maybe he could take all four of us."

Mr. Otterson greeted me at the door and tried his best to set me at ease. Tongue-tied, I could only nod or shake my head. My end of the conversation left something to be desired. He led the way to our seats at one of the gleaming white tables. I found myself gaping at the sparkling goblets, the shining silver service, and the vases of red and white carnations. Mother would have loved the beautiful flowers.

I managed to eat without spilling too much of my food. When some of the brown gravy dripped on the table cover I tried to cover it with my plate. I did drop my spoon just before the ice cream was served and it clattered on the uncarpeted floor. I started under the table to retrieve it, but Mr. Otterson whispered, "Leave it be. We'll get you another." A hard, oval-shaped roll covered with sesame seed had me baffled for a time. I attempted to bite from it as from an apple, but my teeth scarcely dented the thing. I carefully set it aside until I noticed that Mr. Otterson broke his into pieces. Mother's biscuits were never that hard, and I felt sorry for whoever had baked them.

After everyone was through eating there was a program. When Mr. Otterson introduced me and asked me to stand up, my chair nearly tipped over backwards and I had to grab for it. The people all clapped and I could feel my ears burn as they reddened. Toward the end everyone joined in singing, "For He's a Jolly Good Fellow." I was sure they meant Mr. Otterson.

Whatever the occasion that took us out on a winter evening, there was always the long walk home in the dark. Street lamps were few and far between. If a boy was alone, it was kind of scary. Sidewalks had long disappeared by midwinter and devious pathways led over hard-packed snowbanks. Footsteps on the crisp snow made an eerie, crunching sound and the edgy lad might glance over his shoulder looking for a phantom follower. Ghostly shadows of fence post and tree, seen in the pale moonlight, gave the illusion of moving. The sudden crisp rifle shot of frost stress would of a certainty quicken the homeward pace.

With company it was different. Then the tendency was to loiter, to admire the myriad of twinkling stars overhead, and to find the Big Dipper. A ring around the moon elicited all kinds of speculation and imaginative tales. The humming song of taut overhead wires in the still, crisp night air was yet another source of wonderment. To Bumpy, the singing wires were Jack Frost's airplane.

11

Growth, Pain, and Heartbreak

The heart can ne'er a transport know/
That never feels a pain.

—GEORGE LYTTLETON
"Song," 1773

FOR youngsters growing up on Bald Hill Creek during the 1920s there was challenge, excitement, and fun. If we were desperately poor, we didn't know it. Father and Mother likely did. Their daily struggle to provide food, shelter, and clothing was hard, but could only have given purpose to their lives. The simple joys they shared with us permitted them sometimes to forget the poverty. If we were happier when we were poorer, we were also younger. Many of the pastimes of the "good old days" may have been devised to escape the hardships.

It wasn't that misery was stranger to us. We had heartaches by the dozen, minor and major. The saving grace for us as youngsters was that our world was too wonderfully exciting for misery to last very long.

Mother was not the worrying kind. Hers was the courage that could reconcile affection and danger. When Del came home grimacing in pain and clutching his right elbow, Mother suspected a broken arm. "Pull it," pleaded Del, "pull it!" The lower arm sagged at a grotesque angle.

Doc Benson suggested the need for X rays and recommended taking Del to Cooperstown, the Griggs County seat, where such equipment was available. Neighbor Wills volunteered to drive his car. Several hours later Father and Del returned. Del's upper arm had been fractured just above the elbow. The entire arm, from shoulder to hand, was held rigid in a metal support frame. It was a heavy and awkward contraption that Del had to tolerate for several weeks. To make matters worse, the partially knit bone had to be rebroken and reset. Eventually the cumbersome cast was removed. Since the injury involved his throwing arm, Del was much concerned whether it would hamper his baseball playing. Fourtunately it did not.

Obie's turn at injury came when the descending edge of a heavy farm wagon box tore a ragged gash in his scalp. That mishap occurred out at Bill Ferris's farm. The inverted wagon box had been propped on stilts for repair and somehow the props were displaced. Fortunately the falling box struck Obie only a glancing blow. Obie was brought home with his head wrapped in a blood-soaked towel. Stout-hearted Mother neither fainted nor panicked. A look convinced her that the gaping wound required stitches, and this time Doc Benson tended the injury.

I was not to escape unscathed in this rash of calamities. I became a casualty of a skiing accident occasioned by my acting the part of a pretentious show-off. Del and I had spent the winter afternoon skiing on a range of hills about a mile and a half from town. The sun that brief midwinter day was tinging the tops of the hills at setting when we started our homeward trek. One delightful slope remained, and if negotiated, would give us a favorable downhill glide in the right direction. It meant steering a precipitous course parallel to a fence line, then zigzagging through an open gate about half way down. Once through the gate, it was clear sailing all the way to the flat below.

Del opted to go first and break a path. I followed in his tracks a short distance behind. An icy spot and then a soft drift caused Del to lose his balance and fall. I had ample time to take a wipeout myself, but chose to bypass the sprawled out Del by steering a tightrope between him and the fence. I had visions of a glorious recovery in time to thread the gate and outdistance hapless Del. I didn't reckon with a fallen and snow-buried fence post lying across my path. I was streaking toward the gate when the tips of my skis struck this unexpected barrier. I catapulted forward through the air and smashed my face against a timber that served as brace for the gatepost. For several minutes I lay stunned in the snow. A perturbed Del finally got me to my feet. Blood had congealed in the cold and covered my battered visage. Del knew that he had to get me home, well over a mile away. Del carried our skis and steadied me at times when I faltered. That last mile seemed without end. Darkness had fallen before we reached home. An apprehensive Mother thawed me out and surveyed the damage. One eye was swollen shut and there was a gash above it. Also, my nose was broken. This we didn't know at the time, and it healed with a noticeable crook. Del reserved this caustic remark until I was quite healed, "Harvey always sticks his nose in my business. Now he can even do it around a corner."

There were other mishaps: Del's bout with blood poisoning after a nail puncture in his knee, Bumpy's bruises from hailstones, a fishhook imbedded in my thumb. All seemed minor compared to tragedies that befell others in and around Hannaford.

We were profoundly distressed over the plight of a young man who suffered the ravages of the then-feared tuberculosis. What had begun as a slight dry cough and apparently ordinary cold had persisted. It was only after a decided weight loss, followed by acute chest pains and coughing, that the poor fellow's ailment was diagnosed as tuberculosis. By that time the disease was in an advanced stage, with the coughing producing hemorrhages of bright red blood from the lungs. Treatment in those days consisted of complete bed rest and plenty of fresh air. To assure the latter, the young man was confined to a ventilated outdoor tent for all but the coldest months of the year. Passing that yard, viewing that forbidding tent, and perhaps hearing the anguished coughing within was torment for me. The heroic treatment proved of little avail. The unfortunate victim died within two years after being stricken.

The entire town was stunned when two of its citizens, inveterate inebriates, drowned in a slough. The two "happy" travelers were crossing the mud pond on a narrow grade when their open Model T went off the road, overturned, and pinned the two—heads down—in the mire. Though the pair had made hard drinking their main pursuit for years, now a host of shining qualities was extolled by their friends. They gave us to understand that the better nature had been shadowed by but one unfortunate weakness.

The baseball-minded of Hannaford, and that included lads growing up on the Bald Hill, were much grieved when Dave Ostby, popular keystone sacker of the Hannaford baseball team, died. He and a lady friend were found dead in the back seat of an automobile parked in lovers' lane. The two had been asphyxiated by carbon monoxide from the car's leaking exhaust.

Hannaford had its residents who lived alone and withdrawn. Too often, perhaps, we passed them by or let them become the target of idle curiosity. Or sometimes, crueler yet, the recluse suffered the slings and arrows of outrageous mockery and ridicule. One such lonely person was a tall, ungainly girl who attended high school in Hannaford. She lived on a farm only a couple of miles from town. School busses were not available to transport students and Tillie daily walked into town for school and home again. Her forlorn figure plodding along the highway that led into Hannaford was a familiar sight. Few passersby offered her a ride. Gaunt, ill dressed, and almost spectral, Tillie went her solitary way. "Highway Tillie," someone called her, and the appelation stuck. Tillie's ghost reappears to haunt those who drive that road who once passed her by.

For boys growing up on Bald Hill Creek, one particular Fourth of July remains sharply etched in mind. The featured attraction in Hannaford that day had been a baseball game. Obie, Del, Bumpy, and I watched the game from our favorite vantage point out beyond third base. The protruding edge of the stone foundation that supported the school's outhouses provided hard seats with back support.

During the game two of Obie's pals, Cliff Hill and "Baaba" Larson, chugged up to the ball park in the Hill family automobile. The vehicle was a one-seat Model T Ford with a box behind. It had a high windshield but no top. Cliff was understandably proud of having been accorded driving privileges. Such a magnanimous gesture on his father's part was rare indeed. Ordinarily, Cliff and Baaba were pedestrians with the rest of us or might count themselves fortunate to share a bicycle.

My brothers and I envied Obie when he was invited to join Cliff and Baaba in the auto to view the rest of the baseball contest. From their lordly perch the three cast disdainful looks upon those lesser mortals whose posteriors rested upon ground or stone. Del glumly ventured these sour grapes: "I'd rather sit on a rock and have it all to myself than be crowded in that hot old car."

After the game Cliff, Baaba, and Obie departed together in the Model T. We learned later that they had decided to drive to a neighboring town. They were returning to Hannaford in the early evening when they noticed that an approaching car was weaving from one side of the road to the other. Suspecting a drunken driver, Cliff pulled over to the right shoulder and stopped. His caution proved of no avail. The swerving car with its incapable or insensible driver zigzagged across the road and struck Cliff's parked vehicle. The impact of the collision caused the windshield to shatter, and a flying splinter of glass penetrated Cliff's left eye. Neither Baaba nor Obie were injured and the inebriated driver emerged from his car unscathed. Doctors were unable to save Cliff's eye.

Childhood diseases in the early 1900s added to parents' worries. Most children caught and survived chicken pox, measles, mumps, and whooping cough. The prevalent attitude among parents seemed to be that certain diseases were inevitable and the sooner the child had them the better. In fact, a child somehow felt cheated if he couldn't boast, "I've had the measles," or "I've had the mumps."

Chicken pox was generally considered a rather trifling affliction, a nuisance almost beneath one's dignity to catch or brag about. Del was mortified when a single pustule appeared on the end of his nose and Mother diagnosed his ailment as chicken pox.

Diphtheria and scarlet fever were something else again. Doctor Benson considered these serious enough to warrant quarantine. Whenever we saw the large red quarantine notice posted on a door, we gave that house a wide berth. Mother seemed quite amused when Del told of crossing the street so as not to pass too close to an isolated house.

First love, with all of its attendant distractions and unbounded misery, came to one lad at the tender age of twelve. The onslaught left me walking on air, completely clear of the everyday. I suspect that I became all looks, silences, and gestures. The object of my affection was a slight freckle-faced girl in my class. Edna was very much the complete scholar, regarded by all her classmates as the smartest kid in our room. When she sensed that I was having difficulty with problems in arithmetic, she shyly offered to help. With fluttery heart, and rendered dumb by her closeness, I found it impossible to more than mumble gratitude.

In an earlier grade I had sat behind her. More than once I had dipped the ends of her flaxen braids in my inkwell and made her cry. She was just a girl to be teased and tormented. Then when we reached sixth grade, I saw that she was lovely. I carried my yearning like Lent, secretly and dumbly. On a valentine made especially for her, I scrawled the words, "I love you." Lacking the courage to sign my name, I signed it, "You know who." In March she died from a ruptured appendix. I cried.

12

Little Blue Angel

TWO church steeples and four grain elevators dominated the skyline of Hannaford in 1920. Both churches were Protestant—Norwegian Lutheran and Presbyterian. The typical Protestant of the twentieth century inherited his religion as he did his politics, though rather more casually. My parents were both of Scandinavian descent and so we found ourselves members of the Lutheran church by accident of birth and continued the tie through habit. The Willses were of Scottish national origin and with others of English background had a similar nebulous attachment to the Presbyterian church.

Father's only day of rest was Sunday and he donned his Sunday-go-to-meeting suit rather grudgingly. He greeted each Sunday service with a sense of surprise and was convinced he was bestowing a favor upon pastor and congregation by attending.

The good people of Hannaford, whichever summoning bell they heeded, felt the degree of responsibility for the church they might have felt toward some aged relative, whose claim was vague but nonetheless compelling.

Mother saw to it that we were faithful in our attendance at Sunday school, only unfeigned illness or severe winter weather keeping us at home. No one ever satisfactorily explained why we went to one church and many of our playmates to the other. The hours for Sunday school and worship service were the only such segregated hours we knew. Even at Christmastime each church had its own program; children were discouraged from attending the program in the church other than their own, so as to be spared the embarrassment of being passed over when the traditional Christmas treats were distributed. Left to their own devices, the children of Hannaford would, I'm certain, have been quite impartial in bestowing their church allegiance. Some of my happiest church experiences as a child were as an invited guest to Youth Activities Night in the Presbyterian church. Time was allotted for games and for working at crafts in the recreation room. Occasionally we would view a feature-length motion picture in the sanctuary.

An unforgettable moment in that fellowship came toward the end of a pleasant evening of activity as we were having lunch. The youth director was about to peel an orange and asked whether anyone present had a pocketknife. I dug into my pocket and proffered my trusty barlow. As the leader accepted it with a grateful word and smile, he announced for all to hear, "And up steps Harvey Sletten, the hero of the bunch." Such moments of personal triumph were rare indeed, and I went home that night with an inner glow.

Everyone, young and old alike, looked forward to the annual Ladies Aid Fall Supper and Auction Sale. Serving would start promptly at five o'clock and continue until everyone had had his fill at the heaped tables. The ladies strove to outdo each other in preparing the tasty dishes that made up the feast. When the last latecomers had pushed themselves away from the groaning board the tables were cleared and readied for the auction sale.

The industrious ladies of Hannaford prided themselves as much on their needlework as on their cooking and baking. The fruits of their labor were on display throughout the Ladies Aid Hall so that prospective buyers might examine the items before they were offered for bidding. Among the many pieces donated were crocheted doilies of every size and shape; colorful embroidered pillowcases, towels, and aprons; needlepoint pillow covers and pictures; "God Bless' Our Home" and Bible verse samplers; and even a quilt or two. The quilts represented cooperative efforts, with several participants determining either "pieced quilt" or "crazy quilt" pattern.

Food items were also put on the auctioneer's block: golden loaves of fragrant bread, mouth-watering buns, tantalizing pies (apple and pumpkin predominating), cakes, jars of pickles, jellies and other preserves, tempting homemade candies (including chocolate fudge, divinity, and taffy), and always some Norwegian specialties (krum kaka, rosettes, sandbakels, fattigmand, kringla, and the renowned lefse).

Genial and voluble Frank Olson lent his talents as auctioneer. His contagious enthusiasm and ready wit made for spirited, competitive bidding. We worked on Father to bid on some of the edibles that took our fancy. Ever-practical Mother was more interested in dish towels and pillowcases. Bidding on our own was, of course, limited to that portion of meager savings that each elected to spend.

At one such affair, Del had his heart set on acquiring a plate of lefse all for himself. His love for lefse had surfaced when our Sunday school teacher asked members of her class what they were thankful for. Del almost disrupted the class when he answered, "I'm thankful for lefse." As we waited for the selling to begin, Del fingered the coins in his pocket. He had thirty-five cents to spend and was grimly determined to make his presence felt when lefse went on the block. Though he had just finished eating all the lefse he could hold, visions of the plateful he hoped to buy were dancing through his head. It quickly became apparent that others shared Del's taste for the Norwegian delicacy. Several plates were sold at prices from seventy-five cents to a dollar. Each time Del had hopefully bid his thirty-five cents. He was beginning to look pretty glum when the last portion was offered.

"What am I bid for this last plate of lefse?" intoned the auctioneer.

"I bid thirty-five cents!" croaked a desperate Del.

"Sold, to the hungry young man down front," barked Frank.

Heads nodded in beaming approval as a jubilant Del rushed forward to claim his prized purchase.

Part of Father's reluctance to attend the Sunday worship service stemmed from the lengthy sermons that were preached. Some members of the congregation slept through this part of the service, but whenever Father's head began to nod, Mother would nudge him into wakefulness.

Once, the preacher launched into a detailed discourse on the twelve disciples. He dwelt in considerable length upon the character and accomplishments of each. The end of the worship hour neared and our garrulous parson had two or three of the apostles to go. "And now we come to Bartholomew. Where shall we set him among the faithful followers?" he asked.

At this point I distinctly heard Father mumble, as he squirmed in his seat, "You can set him here; I'm going home."

Relaxed at home in his favorite chair, after suffering through one of the extended and often musty sermons, an aggrieved Father would often give vent to injured feelings. He definitely felt put upon. "I don't think the preacher hears himself," Father would grumble.

"If you counted the words that might have been spared, he would have been through in five minutes."

Mother would gently remind Father that the preacher's words were usually fitted to the reflected mood of the hearers.

Word must have gotten back to our pastor that his often recycled sermons were not in particular favor, for he issued the congregation a challenge. Henceforth, any member could write a suggested topic on a piece of paper and leave it on the pulpit. The confident preacher vowed that he would therewith make a sermon from it though the suggestion be but a single word. He was as good as his word, and most admitted to an improvement. One morning a wag (I don't think it was Father) left a blank piece of paper on the pulpit. Undaunted, the preacher remarked, "God created the world out of nothing," and he proceeded to expound for a full hour upon the story of the Creation.

Dull as some of those sermons must have been, church services were not without their lighter moments. Our pastor could wax both eloquent and forceful, often adding emphasis to his words by vigorously pounding his clenched fist on the pulpit. In the middle of one of his impassioned deliveries he thundered, "Who created this world? I ask you, who created this world?" Upraised fist descended, wham! We saw him pale and wince in pain. He gingerly plucked a thumb tack from the heel of his hand, musing aloud, "I suppose it was one of those awful confirmation kids."

Father declared that he wouldn't have missed that Sunday morning in church for anything.

One cold Sunday morning in midwinter, I participated in a strange and memorable drama. The year was 1922. I was only a ten-year-old boy at the time, but the picture is still vividly impressed on my mind. It is as though it happened only yesterday.

The early arrivals for Sunday school at our steepled little church were encouraged to cluster around the hot-air register until the inside temperature permitted classes to begin. The large floor grill of the register was located near the center of the sanctuary. A high, vaulted ceiling arched overhead and doubtless compounded the heating problem.

Sweaters and stocking caps were part of the winter attire for both girls and boys. Small tufts of wool yarn were easy to pluck from sweater or cap, and before long a myriad of varicolored wisps were airborne, darting upward on the thermal air currents. It became a contest to see whose voyageur would ascend the highest and remain afloat the longest.

All too soon a tap on a little bell would summon us to class, while errant bits of fluff still pursued their erratic courses as if taunting us floor-bound mortals.

The morning worship service followed Sunday school. Often it was with some reluctance that we would join our parents in their chosen pew. Sermons were usually lengthy and held little interest for boys with visions of sledding or skating dancing in their heads.

On that particular morning an air of solemnity hung over the congregation. It stemmed from a somber realization that promised financial support for young Mark Thorson's work in a foreign mission field had fallen far short of the needed amount. Mark was popular in our community. He was fresh out of seminary and eager to follow the Lord's calling. In response to heartfelt commiseration by well wishers that morning, Mark was overheard to say, "I guess I'll just have to talk to the Lord some more."

Almost everyone in the little congregation had pledged what they were able toward Mark's mission support—everyone, that is, except Henry Wigen. Henry was beyond doubt the most prosperous individual in the community, but generosity was not one of his recognizable traits. Indeed, Henry was noted for his readiness to quote those sayings of Benjamin Franklin that preached the virtues of industry, frugality, and thrift. "God helps them that help themselves" had sustained Henry and his pocketbook in more than one crisis of conscience. His weekly contribution for the Lord's work, a silver dollar, was placed in the collection plate with an air of finality and resignation. We youngsters fully expected to see him one day remove change.

Besides his natural adverseness to giving, Henry took an equally dim view of a young man with promising business acumen harkening to a rather nebulous call to save heathen souls in far-off places.

In this atmosphere of uncertainty and gloom the service began. The pastor's opening prayer was eloquent and confident—the Lord would open the door for Mark—but in this case no one in the congregation was too hopeful. We all joined lustily in the singing of a hymn; a segment of the lyrics came out strongly, "You shall freely of your gold and silver give." Through it all Henry Wigen sat impassively, hands clasped across his expansive waistline. His jacket was unbuttoned, and from my vantage point I could see the massive gold watch chain that dipped across his vest.

The minister had chosen for a part of his text: "Go ye into all the world and preach the gospel," Mark 16:15. No stone was to be left unturned in the effort to justify Mark's "calling" for Mr. Wigen's benefit. As our earnest pastor proceeded in his own inimitable, ponderous style to develop this directive of the Lord, a few heads started to nod. As he usually did, Henry Wigen went to sleep. After several perfunctory jerks, his head sank slightly forward and came to rest, propped securely by an ample double chin making contact with chest. An almost audible sigh ran through the congregation. Was this powerful exhortation from the pulpit to fall on "ears that heard not?"

Out of nowhere and into my line of vision came floating a tiny wisp of blue wool. For a few moments it paused in its flight, suspended almost motionless midway between ceiling and floor. I noted with a bit of apprehension that it was the same light shade of blue as my sweater. Now it moved majestically upward and to the right a few feet. Then it started a fluttering descent, only to be caught again by a tiny updraft. Ever so gently it was wafted hither and thither. Soon almost every eye was following the graceful undulation of this tiny pilgrim. Only Henry Wigen slept on, oblivious to the overhead drama unfolding before wondering eyes. The airy bit of blue fluff had moved now almost directly over Henry's head. The preacher had launched into the second part of his sermon—this text also had been chosen to reinforce the assault on Henry's purse strings. "A servant of the Lord is worthy of his hire," Luke 10:7. He paused in midsentence, his eyes now riveted on the bit of blue wool. It moved as if guided, closer and closer to Henry Wigen's glistening bald pate. A stray sunbeam from far overhead suddenly highlighted a spot on the top of Henry's head. Gently, ever so gently, almost imperceptibly, the bit of blue gossamer touched down and came to rest.

A tittering broke the silence and spread through the sanctuary. Even the preacher was smiling broadly. To the awakening Henry, the benign smile from the pulpit seemed to be directed at him alone. Faces of those seated in front of him were also turned toward him and smiling. Henry glanced to his left, he glanced to his right, he even turned completely around and looked behind—everywhere people were smiling at him.

In one of those sweeping glances, Mr. Wigen's eyes briefly met mine and I guiltily wondered if he recognized my grinning, jug-eared face as belonging to one of the urchins that each summer he frequently chased out of his strawberry patch.

From his reaction, I can only conjecture at the thoughts that must have flashed through his mind: "Why they're smiling at me!

They like me! They're my friends and neighbors and they like me—even that grinning little rascal. Why, many is the time I'd have spanked him good! They are my brothers!''

A flood of kindliness swept over and engulfed Henry. Basically, he was at heart a very lonely man and he yearned to be loved. Somehow his actions had always erected a seemingly impenetrable wall between him and others. Now amazingly that wall was gone. Henry Wigen had never felt so congenial. Suppressed love flowed forth from him and met a ready response. The wonderful warmth of Christian fellowship overwhelmed him.

The rest is anticlimactic. At the end of the closing prayer Henry's voice joined others in a loud and fervent "Amen." His eyes were suspiciously moist as he pumped every outreached hand and exchanged kindly greetings.

We learned later that Henry had a long and earnest discussion with young Mark Thorson. A week later the congregation wished Mark "Godspeed" as he departed for his great adventure.

Members of our little church shared mixed thoughts about the "miracle" we had witnessed. Some gave credit to Mark's talks with the Lord. To a boy of ten, it was easy to think that he had had a little part in promoting celestial intervention.

Was the re-creation of Henry Wigen complete? I guess only the good Lord could answer that. He continued his accustomed frugal giving, each Sunday morning parting with one silver dollar, always with the same air of finality and resignation. I never did see him remove change.

I can vouch that Mr. Wigen's new congeniality stopped short of his garden gate. The very next summer he caught me in his strawberry patch and whaled me good.

13

The Prisoner
and the Sheriff's Wife

HANNAFORD had its share of singular people. Some may have regarded them as town characters. Certainly these eccentrics were extraordinary, and all were fascinating to a lad growing up on Bald Hill Creek.

Tom Olson was the sexton of our church. We saw him mostly on Sundays when engaged in his official duties. Always he was dressed in somber black, which only enhanced his melancholy nature. A handlebar moustache lent a fierce appearance to his craggy countenance. I know he was a kindly man, for he often opened the heavy outer door of the church for us as we arrived for Sunday school. In wintertime he would help the youngest children unbuckle their overshoes, and if it was a bitterly cold morning, he herded us down to the hot air register to warm us up.

About halfway through our Sunday school hour we could look back into the entryway and see Tom's angular figure bobbing rhythmically up and down as he tugged on the tower bell rope, ringing the bell for the morning service. The bell had a joyous peal as it summoned Sunday morning worshippers. The tolling of the bell at funerals was also Tom's lot. There was only sadness in that sound— the strokes uniformly repeated at intervals. We just knew that it took agonizing effort for Tom to toll a friend's death.

Tom's finest hour came once a year when he marched forward at the end of the children's Christmas program to light the wax candles on the tall Christmas tree that stood at the front of the church. He carried a lit taper on the end of a rod which could be extended to reach the uppermost branches. Tom performed this task with all the majesty of a king wielding his scepter. He moved slowly and deliberately around the tree, touching the tiny flame to each wick in turn. Some seemed reluctant to burst into flame, but under Tom's deft touch every candle was soon burning steadily. Under Tom's watchful eye the candles were allowed to burn while sacks of candy and apples were distributed. Then each candle in turn was carefully snuffed out.

We knew that Tom dug the graves in the cemetery—that in itself made him a lonely and mysterious figure. It gave one a creepy feeling to see him trudging toward the cemetery with the tools of his trade, a spade and pick, across his shoulder.

The fact that Tom was a bachelor and lived alone in a big house added to the mystique. Youngsters gave the lonely house a wide berth whenever an errand or play took them near it. Otto Olson, a shy pal of Obie's, was not related to Tom, but occasionally helped him care for the church property, particularly in mowing the lawn and shoveling the sidewalks. Because of this working relationship, he knew more about Tom than did most of the townspeople.

Otto whetted our curiosity by telling us of the marvelously exciting old automobile that Tom kept hidden away under lock and key in his garage. Otto said that Tom had bought the car many years before to impress a young lady he was courting. When she jilted him and married another man, Tom put the vehicle up on blocks and hadn't used it since. I, for one, wanted very much to get a glimpse of this car. Passing by Tom's yard at a discreet distance, Del and I noticed a couple of small windows in his garage. We also observed that the garage stood well back in the yard, some distance from the house. Certainly a peek through those windows would do no harm.

Caution overcame valor, however, and we decided to do our investigating when Tom was away from home. Casual surveillance paid off. One day Del spotted Tom leaving with his grave-digging tools and we hurried over to his place, making a beeline for the garage. Each of us at a window, we were standing with noses pressed against the dusty glass, peering through cupped hands into the murky interior, when we were suddenly made aware of another presence. We leapt back as a sonorous voice startled us, "Well, well, what have we here?" Tom had returned. Amusement twinkled in his eyes as he beheld our consternation. "Can you see anything in there?" he asked. Tongue-tied, Del and I could only shake our heads.

"So, you want to see my automobile, hah! Come on then, boys, I show you."

Tom unlocked and opened wide the big door, letting the sunlight stream in. There in all its glory stood a polished beauty. Del and I could only gasp our amazement. A fond owner's pride was in Tom's voice as he extolled the merits of his venerable horseless carriage. Tom's automobile was a 1909 Model T Ford. It was a two-seater, with a cloth top that folded back. The shiny black exterior paint and black leather uphostery tended to accentuate the polished brass accouterments up front. The radiator frame, headlight rims, and windshield frame and braces were all of gleaming brass.

We no longer felt like trespassers and Del ventured to ask, "Don't you ever drive it, Mr. Olson?"

Mr. Olson chuckled as he replied, "I intend to, my boy, I intend to—as soon as gasoline goes down to ten cents a gallon."

"Do you think it ever will?" queried incredulous Del. Gasoline at the time was selling for about eighteen cents a gallon.

"It had better, son, it had better—or I'll just get me a horse again."

Mr. Olson was still chuckling as Del and I thanked him and made our departure.

Johnny Sorenson was a happy blond giant in his early twenties who worked as a clerk at the Mercantile General Store. His sunny disposition endeared him to the hearts of young and old alike. Scrupulously honest in his merchandising, Johnny never misrepresented his wares. If fresh frozen fish were no longer fresh, Johnny would tell you; if a jar of butter was suspect, he would caution against buying it. Time after time I saw Mother deliberately stall if Johnny was occupied with another customer. "I'm going to just look a bit," she would say sweetly when another clerk offered his help. I suspect Mother was not alone in employing this artifice.

Johnny was my favorite clerk also. He seemed genuinely glad to see me whether I was on a shopping errand for Mother or on my own. It mattered not if I had only a penny to spend. Johnny's deferential treatment made me feel that I was a mighty important customer. He never hurried me at the glass candy case, but waited patiently as I wrestled with weighty decisions. Ah, the tantalizing choices offered a lad with a coin of the realm clutched in grubby hand. A penny would buy, among other delights, a jawbreaker, a goodly stick of licorice, several peppermints, or a chance on some free pieces of Flinch. Flinch was a trade name for a rather tasteless taffylike candy. It was difficult stuff to either bite or chew and should have made a tempted buyer *flinch*. Its fatal attraction lay in the gamble involved. Each piece of Flinch was individually wrapped and if the word FREE appeared on the inner wrapper, it was just that—free. That entitled the fortunate buyer to select another piece. With a run of luck, the purchaser might acquire several of these flat morsels for his precious penny. Johnny was the only clerk who would take the entire box of Flinch out from the case and permit me to make my own pick. I felt cheated when another clerk handed me one piece and it turned out to be a dud. Johnny shared my disconsolation if I didn't draw at least one free Flinch.

Sometimes I had a whole nickel to spend. Then the choice broadened to include the shelf of five-cent candy bars. These were of goodly size and guaranteed to satisfy a growing lad's sweet tooth. My preference among the nickel treats narrowed down to two, the King Tut and the Fat Emma. I'm quite certain that Johnny may have watched my mouth drool as I deliberated.

Since Johnny was the junior clerk in terms of both age and service, he was often assigned tasks of cleaning, unpacking and stocking, and carrying out. He seemed to relish the carryout, as it gave him the opportunity to exhibit his vaunted strength. Johnny could flip a hundred-pound sack of flour up to his broad shoulder with no visible effort. He was proud of his bulging biceps and eager to share his activities for physical fitness with youths of the community.

One corner of the store's basement had been converted by Johnny into a gymnasium of sorts. Here he practiced weight lifting, both with barbell and pulley weights. He skipped rope and worked out with punching bags. Every Friday night during the winter his gym was open to interested boys. Del and I struggled mightily with the barbell weights and attempted to catch and throw the unwieldy medicine ball. We battered our knuckles against the ponderous, swinging sandbag with little avail. In each activity Johnny instructed and encouraged. We all learned that we must abide by two inflexible rules. Johnny would tolerate neither swearing nor roughhousing. He encouraged fun, but it had to be good clean fun.

All of us were amazed and delighted when one night Johnny danced the Charleston for us. The year was 1925 and this lively dance was sweeping the country at the time. Johnny soloed through its wild gyrations to the music of a phonograph. His long legs performed unbelievable contortions, with much knee and ankle twisting, and with both feet moving simultaneously into a pigeon-toed stance, heels flung alternately outward. His arms tried to keep pace, furiously and rhythmically crisscrossing in front of his body. The all-out effort left Johnny perspiring and panting.

A set of boxing gloves was available and at times some of the boys wanted to exhibit their pugilistic prowess. Johnny discouraged mismatches, whether by age, size, or skill. He was quick to stop a match if tempers flared or bodily harm was apparent. Del reveled in the sport and was an aggressive fighter. I did not share his enthusiasm for boxing and tried to avoid being involved. One night, however, I was egged into putting on the gloves with Mike Cook. Mike was about my age and size, though somewhat stronger. We jabbed away at each other for awhile without either having any particular advantage. Del and others started heckling and urging a little action. All of a sudden, caution abandoned, Mike and I were slugging it out, toe-to-toe. Mike let one fly, right from the shoulder, busting me in the mouth and sending me reeling across a bench. Johnny intervened immediately, but the damage was done. The sturdy blow had chipped the biting edge off one of my front teeth. An unpromising boxing career had been nipped in the bud.

No one knew what had brought Nate Cotton and his young wife to Hannaford nor where they had hailed from. They got off the train one day and stayed. To our knowledge, black men were either porters on trains or traveling baseball players. In view of his grizzled hair, we judged Mr. Cotton too old to be a baseball player. The Cottons had checked in at the California House and, the story had it, after sampling a few meals cooked by California Hans, Mr. Cotton decided that Hannaford's immediate and pressing need was a new eating establishment. The townsfolk agreed and welcomed the business venture with open hearts and grateful stomachs.

Cotton's Restaurant and Soda Fountain soon gained a reputation as a first-class public eating house. The clientele consisted of regular boarders, quickly recruited from those long disenchanted with the bill of fare at the California House, plus the ever-present drummers making their rounds. Family dining-out was an infrequent occurrence, even for the affluent.

Customers had only one unhappy adjustment to make. At irregular intervals they would find Cotton's place locked up. The next day would be business as usual, except that Mrs. Cotton's face often bore the bruises of recent battle. The eaters could only surmise that Nate was the master of his household. The town gossips interjected that elderly Mr. Cotton needed to keep his attractive young wife in line.

Hannaford's youngsters were not long in determining that Mr. Cotton dished out the biggest ice cream cones to be had anywhere.

Either they had a generous fringe to be licked off or else were topped with a minidip over the regular scoopful.

Occasionally as Del and I trudged the banks of the Bald Hill on a fishing expedition, we would come upon Mr. Cotton sitting on the grassy bank with a line in the water. Invariably he was fishing for and catching bullheads, which really didn't qualify him as a fisherman in our eyes. We were dumfounded when we saw him catch and release a pike. He told us that while the bullheads couldn't compare to good old Mississippi River catfish, they were still mighty good eating.

California Hans evinced no animosity toward his Johnny-come-lately competitor. He continued as the indifferent proprietor of the California House, a ramshackle rooming house and hostelry. The diminished demand for his meals gave him more time for drinking, which now became almost a full-time pursuit.

Hannaford's town marshal of many years was one of the permanent roomers at the California House. Marshal Hanson ("Ole" to his friends) took a tolerant view toward imbibers and bootleggers. Moonshiners operated with impunity in Ole's bailiwick until the "Feds" started nosying around. Ole was not beyond taking a nip himself, and this apparently endeared him to the all-male electorate. It was scarcely surprising that Ole became one of Hannaford's first casualties of woman suffrage.

Ole's sole claim to fame could be accredited to his encounter with an apparent burglar as he made his haphazard rounds late one night. Investigating a noise to the rear of the Mercantile Store, Ole spied a dim figure emerging from an opened window. It was then that Ole is said to have uttered his immortal command, "You yump vunce, you yump no more." A loaded shotgun backed up Ole's ultimatum.

"Don't shoot, Ole, don't shoot! It's me, Tom. I won't jump—just help me down."

Ole recognized the voice of a fellow roomer from California House. The prowler had his arms full of lemon and vanilla extract. Activities of federal agents had dried up local supplies and Tom had an overpowering thirst to assuage.

"Jazzy" Wigen had acquired notoriety as a gambler while he was yet in school. More than once an exasperated teacher had confiscated either cards or dice. Lectures on the evils of gambling and admonishment alike fell on deaf ears as far as Jazzy was concerned. Mothers complained about "that Wigen boy"—that he was a bad influence on other boys in the school. Jazzy's father was on the school board and some of the complainers thought Mr. Wigen used his position to keep his erring son in school.

Jazzy was not above seeking help from classmates on assignments he had neglected to complete or on tests he found himself unprepared for. Often Obie was the one to whom Jazzy turned in such moments of desperation. Jazzy was not altogether ungrateful for such favors and on one occasion rewarded Obie by giving him a handsome pair of red celluloid dice. I don't think that Obie knew exactly what they were used for except that they were something to carry and admire. At times he would condescend to let Del and me handle and examine them. "What are they good for?" a puzzled Del asked.

"Give 'em here—I'll show ya," was Obie's diffident reply. He cradled the cubes in cupped hands and blew noisily on them. "Seven come eleven," he intoned, as with a flourish he let the dice tumble on the floor.

"What for?" Del was insistent. "What d'ya want seven to come eleven for?"

" 'Cuz that's what ya need to win, Stupid."

"To win what?"

Obie shrugged, pocketed the mysterious "galloping dominos," and stalked off in a quandary.

Our fascination with Obie's dice was short-lived. They mysteriously disappeared and Obie didn't seem too unhappy. I suspect that Mother may have been involved in the vanishing act. From the outset, she had viewed Obie's acquisition with a marked lack of enthusiasm.

Jazzy's nefarious extracurricular activities came more and more into disfavor with school authorities and patrons alike, and he was persuaded to drop out of school. I am certain that this arrangement was to Jazzy's liking. He could now devote full time to his gaming. There were dark whispers of the poker games that went on in a back room of the California House. Always Jazzy was mentioned as the promoter of these high-stake games. Rumors persisted that Jazzy fleeced inept local gamesters and visiting drummers alike. The illicit poker games became a precarious undertaking after the women electorate unseated Marshal Ole Hanson. Under Ole's benign jurisdiction the gamblers had felt secure, knowing that Ole would warn them of the sheriff's imminence. Ole's successor cooperated with the sheriff and periodically the games were raided. In an effort to baffle the law, location of the game was put on a floating basis. On one occasion, the sheriff and the marshall took eight men in hand as a result of a raid upon a barn where gambling was in progress.

A fiery cross burning at night atop the bluff overlooking the Bald Hill left a frightened citizenry speculating as to whom this sinister warning was directed. The year was 1924. Father and Mother spoke guardedly of a mysterious Ku Klux Klan— masked and white-robed men who flogged, lynched, and tortured people they did not like. Whatsoever the portent of the burning cross, the lawless element of Hannaford may have been intimidated more by the moral outrage of the women.

The inevitable finally happened. Jazzy was accused of dealing cards off the bottom of the deck and was threatened by a transient roustabout known as "Big Jess." Everyone agreed that Big Jess was not a man that would take cheating lightly—he was a bad one to mess around with. Jazzy must have entertained the same disturbing thought, for he hastily packed a bag and skipped town. The self-righteous citizens of Hannaford emitted a collective sigh of relief. The fledgling den of the Ku Klux Klan folded its robes and died prematurely.

Abbie Lucas was a promoter of nefarious schemes—always with someone else's money. His large family saw little of him, for Abbie's promotions kept him on the move. A mere look from Abbie's bold eyes could cause even the staid president of the Ladies Aid to blush and tremble. He had a way with women, that handsome rascal. Even the county jail could not long contain Abbie, with the sheriff's wife bringing his meals.

Abbie had the audacity to undertake anything, and he was a spellbinder. One thing that held no appeal for Abbie was a steady job. He firmly believed his talents were deserving of more latitude than laboring specific hours would permit. As a result, his family was often destitute. On at least one occasion sympathizers felt obliged to take up a collection for Mrs. Lucas. California Hans spearheaded the drive for funds and was the largest contributor. Ironically, he was one of those Abbie turned in when he was working for the Feds during prohibition. Because of Abbie's duplicity, the local supply of illegal liquor was effectively curtailed for a time.

Disgruntled drinkers marched on his house intent on a lynching party. Somehow, advance warning had reached Abbie, which prompted him to leave town.

Always Abbie dreamed of the big kill, of making a fortune through his wits. He had proved beyond doubt that he could sell. He was a very persuasive man, often hiding under his tongue. He was a flashy dresser, and attired in his gray Prince Albert with its distinctive velvet lapels, bowler worn at a jaunty angle, gray spats accentuating gleaming black boots, he looked every inch the successful business tycoon.

At one time Abbie came up with an ingenious metal pants hanger which he tried to manufacture and market. He was able to acquire a partner who was willing to invest a few thousand dollars in the spring steel and wire required. The relatively simple assembly was undertaken at night in hotel rooms. Abbie experienced no trouble in selling the device, which appeared quite useful. Slipped within the bottoms of the trouser legs, it preserved a semblance of press and provided for hanging. As usual, however, success seemed to elude Abbie. While in his mind he was actively organizing a thriving business enterprise, even to the extent of promising high positions in the company to his friends, he failed to attract the capital necessary for large-scale production. His Little Jiffy Pants Hanger empire proved but another will-o'-the-wisp.

Undaunted, Abbie looked for bigger fields to conquer. He soon hooked up with a notorious swindler in an oil well drilling scheme. This big-time operator may well have been out of Abbie's league. The clever promoter had already interested enough backers that he had actually started to drill a well. Abbie's job was to use his eloquence in luring additional potential investors to the well site for an on-the-spot come-on. A fleet of Model T Ford touring cars were used to haul the eager suckers to the scene of operations. They were wined and dined and even housed overnight, all the time mesmerized by the relay sales pitch of these two accomplished rascals. The clincher came when liquid fuel, apparently drawn directly from the unfinished oil well, was poured into the tanks of the Model T Fords. The engines were cranked and performed admirably on even this unrefined petroleum. Astonished and impressed, the observers were more than ready to pull out their checkbooks and get in on the promised ground floor.

It was only a matter of time until the sheriff came looking for Abbie. His erstwhile partner had absconded with the loot. Abbie was held on a charge of obtaining money under false pretenses.

To be incarcerated was not a new experience for Abbie. He regarded a sojourn in the hoosegow as only a temporary inconvenience, a calculated risk to be accepted with good grace. Stone walls did not a prison make, nor iron bars a cage for Abbie's scheming mind. Cheerful and resigned, he was already envisioning new projects, new worlds to conquer. Prospects took a definite turn for the better when the sheriff's wife appeared with Abbie's supper. In their mutual appraisal, each perceived in the other an exciting challenge. The pair had supplementary talents. She reveled in playing the coquette, and as a philanderer Abbie had no peer. Though the contest started on even terms, Cupid's odds were riding on smooth-tongued Abbie. Under the spell of his honeyed words, the erstwhile siren became as butter.

Before a week had passed Abbie held undisputed sway over the heart of this coquette. It may have been his finest performance as a trifler. Winning a thousand common hearts entitled Abbie to some renown. Winning the heart of the sheriff's coquettish wife established him as a hero. They "flew the coop" together.

14

Work Binds the Free

*Who first invented work and bound the free/ And
holiday-rejoicing spirit down?*

—CHARLES LAMB
"Work," 1819

CAREFREE summers came to an abrupt end for us as soon as we
were old enough to be farmed out. Grim necessity required that we
become productive members of the family to whatever extent we
could. If Mother's wishes on schooling were to be acceded to, Father
was equally determined that we seek after-school and Saturday odd
jobs and such summer employment as were offered.

Our first work experience of any duration was a ten-day stint of
tramping fields of growing grain and pulling wild mustard plants. In
the early summer of 1921 Obie, Del, and I became part of a work
crew of fifteen or twenty youngsters recruited by a nearby farmer for
this task. We were each paid ten cents an hour. We walked the two
and one-half miles to the farm each morning and home again in late
afternoon. Our actual workday in the fields averaged five or six
hours. Our work was directed by a young man who acted as
foreman. He kept us spaced and moving across the field and back in
measured laps. An accumulated armful of the leafy plants was
carried until it could be deposited in a dead furrow.

The shortest route from Hannaford to the farm was "as the
crow flies." This entailed crossing Bald Hill Creek on the long
wooden railroad trestle that spanned the valley. One morning as we
hurried toward our work rendezvous, a freight train had stopped on
the edge of town and its string of cars extended across and well
beyond the bridge. A narrow walkway permitted single-file passage
alongside the standing train. With little hesitation the other
youngsters, led by Del, undertook the precarious crossing. Only I
was chicken. I had disturbing thoughts of the train starting up while

we were on the bridge. Our proximity to the moving cars could make one misstep fatal.

I chose to stay on terra firma and follow a footpath down into the valley. I knew I could cross the creek on stones about a mile downstream. By now the rest were safely on the other side and ready to cut cross-country. Obie was furious. I knew he was torn between continuing on with the others or sticking with me. My elected route would of a certainty put us well behind the others. I moved at a trot along my side of the creek with Obie keeping pace on the other and upbraiding me at every step. He stuck with me all the way to the ford. Once across, I discretely followed a surly Obie on our backtracking roundabout trek.

Nothing was said about this episode to Father or Mother. We were well aware that the short cut via the railroad trestle may not have been a parentally approved route.

We were encouraged to wear shoes in the fields to protect our feet from thorns and thistles. I was breaking in a bargain-counter pair of buttoned yellow shoes. They hurt my feet, and one morning as we started pulling mustard I decided to remove the tormenting footgear and work barefooted. Looking around for a place to leave the shoes, I spotted a gang plow standing near the corner of the field. Satisfied that this landmark would be easy to spot for later retrieval, I placed the shoes in a furrow ahead of the implement. At the end of the day I went to get my shoes. The plow was gone—my shoes buried in an unmarked grave.

A dazed look spread over Father's face as I tried to explain the missing shoes. "You . . . you . . . you what?" he stammered. Patiently I repeated the sorry tale. Father's head wagged slowly in wondering disbelief. Glassy-eyed, he mumbled something unintelligible and stalked out of the room.

When the mustard pulling was completed, the hours worked were added up. Obie, Del, and I together had a total of 158 hours. A check in the amount of $15.80 was made out to Father. Three jubilant boys could scarcely wait to get home with the hard-earned money. To us it was a truly impressive sum.

The following summer I hired out to herd cows on Uncle Chet's farm. The agreed wage, approved by Father, was to be ten dollars a month plus keep. Herding cows on the prairie day after day proved a lonely task for a ten-year-old boy. Many things could be learned out there, but I found it such a solitary classroom. Even though Uncle Chet's farm was only six miles from Hannaford, I got home for brief visits only two or three times during the summer. My thoughts turned often to happier times on Bald Hill Creek—the old swimming hole, fishing along its grassy banks, the endless succession of baseball games. Whenever the homesickness became acute, I found solace in an airy retreat high in the branches of a willow tree. A clump of the tall willows grew in a remote part of the farmyard. My tree seemed built for climbing. I was able to mount from limb to limb until I clung swaying at the very pinnacle. My lofty perch became a crow's nest high on the mast of a tossing clipper. From my lookout I could spot Uncle Chet's Grant touring car approaching when he was yet a couple of miles away. Dropping swiftly to the ground, I would race to the house to convey the news to Aunt Christy and Grandma Wunderlich.

The glorious Fourth of July was viewed as a welcome break by farm folk. It separated two work seasons. Planting was usually completed by mid-June and haying began in earnest right after the Independence Day celebration. The lull between might well be taken up by dipping into the reservoir of stored-up tasks, including fence mending.

My Uncle Carl and his wife Anna lived in the nearby town of Dazey. Uncle Carl was the genial proprietor of the Pleasant Rest Hotel and Pool Emporium. Uncle Carl and Aunt Anna kindly offered to take me with them to the Fourth of July celebration at Valley City. Uncle Chet gave me a dollar for spending money.

The morning of the 4th, 1922, dawned bright and sunny. I needed no urging to get up and fetch the cows for the morning milking. I gulped down my breakfast and donned my best shirt and pants. The comforting feel of the silver dollar in my pocket lent urgency to my impatience to be on our way.

Uncle Chet delivered me to Dazey. To ride up front with him in the luxurious Grant touring car was a thrill in itself. We pulled up in front of the Pleasant Rest in grand style and I transferred to the back seat of Uncle Carl's less pretentious Model T. The thirty-mile ride to Valley City over a hot and dusty road seemed endless. Bouncing all over that back seat, I clutched my precious dollar throughout the journey.

I was my own man for the day once we arrived in Valley City. Uncle Carl dropped me off near the ball park, where a carnival was set up. I had often heard Father proclaim that a fool and his money are soon parted. In a relatively short time I became painfully aware that this time I had played the fool. With the exception of a nickel spent for an ice cream cone, I had squandered my money on a wheel of fortune. A plaster Kewpie doll, garishly attired in a brief costume of brilliant orange-colored feathers was my dubious trophy. The barker running the game made the most of my winning. Waving the dazzling prize on high, he whooped at the top of his voice, "Lookie, lookie, look what he won!" Embarrassed by the good-natured smiles of onlookers, I quickly departed the place. I regretted mightily having spent my dollar so quickly and foolishly, but found some consolation in the thought that Mother might like the doll for her dresser. She had so few pretty things.

The day had kind of come and gone for me. I endured an interminable wait for Uncle Carl and Aunt Anna. By the time they picked me up in late evening I was both hungry and tired. I had resolved to put up a brave front and assured them that I had enjoyed a wonderful day. It happened that My Uncle Lefty had also spent the day celebrating in Valley City. Uncle Carl, in his role as brother-in-law, felt a responsibility to see that Uncle Lefty got home. Uncle Lefty was gloriously drunk, and it was almost midnight before Uncle Carl could drag him from the speakeasy where he had spent most of the day carousing with his buddies. Uncle Lefty needed help to stumble into the back seat where I had been curled up sleeping. I awoke enough to realize with dismay that we would share the seat for the long trip home.

By the time the gallant Model T had chugged and sputtered its way up the winding hill to the flat above, rain had started to fall. Uncle Carl stopped and put on side curtains.

Uncle Lefty had passed out and his raucous snores reverberated in my ear. His sprawling body rolled with the jolting Model T and at times his inert weight crushed almost full upon me. Intermittent flashes of lightning lit up the water-filled ruts ahead. That was about all Uncle Carl had to steer by. The night was very black, and the flickering headlights, powered by the Model T's magneto, dimmed or rose with the faltering engine. The side curtains kept out only a part of the rain. Sheer exhaustion mercifully permitted fitful sleep. I dozed. In my dreams the wheel of fortune went round and round.

I awakened to the sound of Aunt Christy's voice calling me. Uncle Carl had carried me into the house and tucked me in. Mother's Kewpie doll, or what was left of it, was on a chair beside my bed. Its plaster head had been broken off during the wild night ride.

Uncle Chet operated a steam threshing rig in the fall. In late summer Father came out to the farm to overhaul and ready the grain separator. With several men involved in the harvesting and preparations for threshing, meals were now served in the cook car. Grandma Wunderlich presided as head cook during the threshing season. It was a thrill for me to join the men at the long tables in this kitchen and diner on wheels.

As we hungrily ate our supper one evening, Father casually announced that it would rain within twenty-four hours. The sky at the time was clear, and I don't think anyone took his prediction too seriously. Twenty-three hours and fifty-five minutes later the sky opened up and we had a deluge. As the rain drummed on the roof of the cook car, someone wonderingly recalled Father's earlier forecast. When asked to explain his augury, a very smug Father stated blandly, "My corns hurt last night. It never fails." Father basked in his moment of triumph.

My cow-herding days on the prairie came to an end when Uncle Chet's cows were sold at a forced auction sale. In my heart I wasn't sorry. In Uncle Chet's absence, which was frequent, I often had to milk the cows alone. When some of the cows went dry sooner than expected, it was easy to put the blame on my inefficient performance of the milking operation.

My next work assignment was for Uncle Lefty. Father must have realized that Uncle Lefty was somewhat less than a dependable employer, but in his determination to lessen demands on his own board, Father saw fit to overlook Uncle Lefty's failings.

Often the work was only to help Aunt Clara with the chores and keep her company. She was left alone a lot, and at times there wasn't too much in the house to eat. When that happened, we would go down to the creek and fish for chub and red horse. These small fish were easily caught and, aside from being bony, were quite tasty when fried to a golden crisp.

At harvesttime I would ride the grain binder behind Lefty's Moline tractor. My job was to raise or lower the reel with a hand-operated lever and to trip the bundle carrier with its foot-operated release. My ineptness on this machine taxed Uncle Lefty's patience beyond the breaking point at times. His often-expressed irritation took any possible joy out of this task.

Sometimes I went with Grandpa Rasmussen to shock the grain. We would drive to the scattered fields in his venerable Buick roadster. Grandpa's inseparable companion, a beautiful black and white collie, rode on the seat between us. Grandpa took pride in setting the shocks of grain firmly and well. I loved to be with him and profited greatly from his kindly wisdom. He took care not to overwork me and we would frequently sit and rest in the partial shade of a grain shock. His faithful dog shared our lunch and drinking water. Grandpa would scoop out a shallow depression in the earth and fill it with water from our jug. During the break, Grandpa would fill his pipe with Prince Albert and puff contentedly while he dispersed his homespun philosophy and tales.

When I was thirteen, Father arranged for me to work during summer vacation for a bachelor who needed someone to do summer plowing for him. I learned to drive five horses, in three-two tandem, ahead of a two-bottom gang plow. It took a little doing to manipulate four driving reins, two in each hand. The tricky part came in turning the rig at the ends of the field. One hand had to be free to work the lever that lifted the bottoms from the ground, and the horses had to be turned properly at the same time. The ends of the field were invariably bounded by fence and this limited the turning area.

On that plow seat I felt mighty grown up—monarch of all I surveyed. One Monday morning I took a newly acquired pipe and a tin of tobacco with me on the plow. On the first few rounds I was in a state of euphoria. Suddenly I became dizzy and then violently sick. When I was finally able to crawl back up on the seat, I tossed pipe and tobacco into the furrow ahead of the plow. How quickly the mighty can fall!

In North Dakota severe thunderstorms can come up suddenly on a hot summer day. One sultry afternoon I kept an apprehensive eye on a rapidly mounting thunderhead. I was plowing nearly a mile away from the farmstead. The ominous buildup prompted me to unhook the five-horse team from the plow and hurry them toward home and shelter. I urged the tired animals to a trot and ran behind them. The first angry drops were spattering as we drew abreast of the barn. A neighbor from across the road had noted my plight and came running to help me unhitch the nervous horses and get them inside the barn. Hailstones were starting to pelt us as we got under cover. The severe hailstorm that followed caused extensive damage to growing crops.

The following summer I went back to work for Uncle Lefty. Basically, Lefty was good-hearted, and I suppose we should have been grateful to him for taking on such a young and untried hired hand. I harbored an unconfirmed suspicion that no one else would work for him. At any rate, Uncle Lefty convinced Father that he needed my help.

I was old enough now to attempt most of the jobs the season demanded. During the haying season I drove a team of horses on the hayrake and worked in the stack when we were stacking. I was raking hay one afternoon when something spooked the horses. I had observed a runaway once at Uncle Chet's farm; it had been a frightening thing to watch. Now, involved myself, I was terrified. The horses bolted across the meadow at a dead run. There was nothing I could do but hang on. The high wheels of the hayrake

Uncle Lefty (standing) with Cousin Alice and Grandpa Rasmussen in his Buick roadster.

Uncle Carl (in vest, tie, and black arm sleevelets) was the genial proprietor of the Pleasant Rest Hotel and Pool Emporium. Drummers and other travelers were overnight guests here and could eat, rest, and enjoy recreation.

Cultivating corn was a demanding early summer job.

Harvey helped shock the grain at harvesttime.

Harvey drove the stacker team when Uncle Chet and Uncle Lefty put up hay.

bounced over rocks and badger holes. I don't know how I managed to stay in the wildly careening seat. The runaway team made a looping circle, then straightened out and headed for home. Nearing the barnyard they headed toward an open gate. One wheel struck and splintered a gatepost. The winded horses slowed to a canter, and I was able to pull them to a trembling stop short of the barn door. An ashen-faced Uncle Lefty grabbed hold of a bridle strap and steadied the skittish animal as I staggered from the seat. Uncle Lefty let me know that I had done a very foolish thing in not bailing out at the start and letting the horses go.

At harvesttime I shocked grain. Wrestling the heavy bundles of grain was hard work for a slightly built lad, even when I rested frequently. Once I incurred Uncle Lefty's displeasure by idling away most of an afternoon picking and eating chokecherries along the nearby creek.

Lefty owned a small threshing rig and threshed grain for some of his neighbors. During threshing I drove Lefty's team and hayrack, hauling bundles. The hayrack, like much of Lefty's farm equipment, was old and rickety. It was difficult to load, for unless weight was distributed evenly throughout the rack, the load threatened to tip over. The other bundle haulers, all with stable equipment, recognized my handicap and sympathized with me. They encouraged me to be satisfied with smaller, lighter loads, even if that added to their own work.

My luck ran out one morning and I tipped a load of spelt. We were hauling the bundles of spelt from a field in the creek bottom, and the prairie trail sloped along the gentle hillside. I was thrown clear of the overturning rack, and my team stopped in their tracks. The wagon's running gear was still in one piece, but I could see that the coupling pole joining the hind axle to the forward part of the wagon was broken and twisted. I decided to leave the overturned rack as it was and take the wagon in for repair of the damaged reach. I walked alongside the wagon and guided the horses. Before I got up to the threshing rig a rear wheel fell off. Somehow, the tipping rack had flipped over the rear axle so that sustained forward movement turned the holding nut off from the axle, permitting the wheel to drop.

Embarrassed, frustrated, and piqued, I announced I was quitting the job then and there. The next morning, wagon operational again, I was hauling bundles as usual. In this case, Father's anticipated displeasure was the tie that binds. I was Lefty's "man Friday," for better or for worse.

Things went from bad to worse for Uncle Lefty in his farm

operation. The last summer I worked for him, he owed me most of my summer wages when I returned home to start school a few weeks late. The sum was modest, seventy-five dollars, but Lefty told Father I would have to wait for my pay until he sold his wheat. Lefty admitted that other creditors were pressing him and he reluctantly agreed to let Father file a labor lien on the crop.

The wearisome monotony of farm work gave way to a different type of toil the summer following my graduation from high school in 1929. I went to work as an extra hand on a railroad section gang. Cousin "Gaga" had the job first but failed to measure up to expectations of the exacting section foreman. After his disappointment with Gaga, the foreman was somewhat less than enthusiastic when I applied for the job. I was perhaps ten pounds lighter than my cousin and quite an unpromising candidate for the grueling work of a track roustabout. I begged to be given a try and the dubious foreman reluctantly agreed.

The work was hard and less than glamorous. Leveling track occupied much of the time, with the tie tamping laboriously done by foot pressure on the heel of a tamping spade. My job was assured when I readily acquired the knack of driving the gravel ballast underneath the upraised wooden sleepers. Tamping was a back-breaking task, and performed under the beating rays of a blazing summer sun could be excruciating torture.

A smudge of black smoke on the shimmering horizon was a most welcomed sight. It signaled the approach of a train and a respite from our toil, because we had to clear the track and await its passage. A long, lumbering freight provided a delightful interlude. A passenger train hurried past with scant regard for our stolen rest.

Indifferent eyes stared down at us from the comfortable confines of the speeding coaches. With weary bodies leaning on our tampers, I'm sure that we bore marked resemblance to Millet's "Man with the Hoe." As Markham described, "Stolid and stunned, a brother to the ox" (Edwin Markham, "The Man with the Hoe, 1899). How I envied the seemingly carefree travelers.

Working on the railroad made me firmly resolve not to condescend to a lifetime of unskilled labor. Father had always tried to impress upon his sons the thought that all work was honorable and worth doing well. I must confess that I found little enobling in that kind of drudgery.

There were a few lighter moments. One week the foreman took us off the track leveling and set us to the somewhat easier task of raking and cleaning tree belts. Hornets' nests abounded in the tangled underbrush. Disturbed, these cantankerous insects could disperse the work crew in short order. On one occasion a horde of the maddened wasps singled out our foreman as the object of their attack. Beating ineffectively at the tormentors with his hat, the beleaguered victim took off running. We watched him take a diving tumble over an embankment. Sliding and rolling down the steep incline to the tracks below, he somehow eluded his angry pursuers. Our subdued foreman suffered a few painful stings and some bruises from his precipitous descent but considered himself fortunate to have escaped so lightly. I would be less than truthful if I didn't admit to a certain vicarious pleasure in the poor man's discomfiture.

And so, if work bound the free, it also made the classroom more appealing. The schoolhouse door looked downright inviting after the summer's toil. Someone asked me once if I was ever tempted as a boy to quit school. The answer, "No." It wasn't that I loved books so much, but that I relished hard, unremitting labor less.

15

"Shorty Long-Pants"

THERE was never a child so lovely but his mother was glad to see him off to school. For boys growing up on Bald Hill Creek, the hardest part of starting school in the fall may have been donning shoes again. Scarred and calloused, the feet that had roamed unfettered all summer protested mightily the torture of footwear. The transition was especially painful if there were new shoes to break in. Mother insisted on all of the buttons being fastened, and the task of drawing buttons through buttonholes with a buttonhook on a pair of new, stiff leather shoes sometimes made getting ready for school a loudly protested affair.

Mother was equal to the task, however, and her children were seldom absent from school or tardy. Somehow, even indolent Del was bustled out the door and on his way in time to get in under the tardy bell. Del had learned early in his first year of school that daily attendance was quite unrelated to his personal inclination. Curiosity had likely prompted him to go willingly on his first day. The second morning Del had apparently decided to put Mother's authority to the test. He dawdled at the breakfast table and lingered at the door, defiant of Mother's prompting. When she reached for her willow switch, Del started on his reluctant way. At the edge of the yard he stopped and eyed Mother, who stood in the doorway monitoring her son's hesitant departure. Willow wand in hand, Mother advanced, and again Del ambled off in the direction of the schoolhouse. Each time Mother stopped, Del also stopped. The slow, relentless pursuit continued all the way to the schoolhouse door. Mr. Sorenson, the school janitor, was sweeping the front steps as the two approached. He took in the situation in a glance. Wise to the ways of schoolboys, Mr. Sorenson said not a word, but his eyes twinkled as he opened the door for Del. Mother had won another round.

Youngsters attending the Hannaford school were vaccinated en masse for smallpox when I was in the third grade. The technique at the time (1920) was quite crude. Doc Benson ruptured the skin on the upper arm by scratching a small area with a sharp-pointed instrument. A smear of cowpox virus was placed on this open wound and a perforated felt plate or washer was taped to the arm to keep clothing from contact with the sore. After an interval of several days Doc returned to see if the vaccination had "taken." Mine apparently was satisfactory. Some of the boys and girls had to submit to the procedure a second time. That kind of vaccination left a scar the size of a dime or larger. We wore the scars proudly and were quite ready to show and compare.

Stories had it that when Doc Benson first started his medical practice, he hauled a trussed-up calf in the back of his buggy to ensure a fresh supply of cowpox virus.

Parents who knew the horrors of a smallpox epidemic welcomed Doc Benson's vaccinations, harsh and uncertain as they were. The faces of some of Hannaford's older residents were horribly pitted and scarred from surviving the ravages of smallpox in their youth. We knew too, that many had succumbed to this dread disease before vaccination became widely known and accepted.

I'm certain that Mother prided herself on sending us off to school with a well-scrubbed and combed appearance. She must have despaired at times the task of getting her brood of five out of bed in the morning, overseeing their dressing, inspecting their washing and combing efforts, and getting them to the breakfast table—all in time to heed the school bell. It could only have been with a deep sigh of relief, and perhaps a degree of disbelief, that she saw the last malingerer depart on time.

Clothing was drab for most of the children in Hannaford. Shapeless ginghams, well-patched overalls, coarse chambray shirts, and shawl-collared, coat-length black or navy blue sweaters made the students quite indistinguishable. Little girls wore their hair in braids or pigtails. As they approached their teens it was usually cut in a straight bob, while the more daring of the high school girls in the middle and late 1920s went for the flapper look and had their hair shingled. Most of the boys parted their hair in the middle and combed it straight down the sides.

Our haircuts were done at home, with Father wielding the scissors and hand clipper. He disdained use of a bowl, maintaining that only a rank amateur needed such an artifice. Father liked a free rein for his tonsorial artistry. He preferred to do all four of us at a sitting. This sometimes led to a little argument as to which one would submit first. I think the feeling was unanimous that the first shearing was the riskiest. Father would be rusty at the job, and, after all, "practice makes perfect." This old adage may not have applied to Father's barbering, however. On occasion, the one holding out for last found cause to lament. Father, warming to his task, may have reserved his greatest zeal for his windup.

Father's barber tools, shears and clipper, I'm certain, dulled over a period of time and sometimes pulled enough to bring a protesting "Ouch, that pulls," or "Ouch! that hurts!" Bumpy seemed to be the most stoic about the discomfort, heroically suppressing any outward manifestation of pain. Del, on the other hand, was the most vociferous in giving vent to his outraged feelings.

Mother was a quiet spectator as one after another of her shaggy-haired sons crawled atop the pile of catalogs on Father's makeshift barber's chair. She viewed the proceeding a bit apprehensively, but saw fit to intervene only when a distinct lopsidedness was evident. If she ventured that one side appeared higher than the other, Father invariably overcorrected. This could go on and on, with disastrous results. Once, after being the victim of this "evening up" process, as he explored the pitiful topknot that remained, Bumpy cheerfully remarked, "Well, at least it'll be easy to comb."

While Father's haircuts may have left something to be desired, some of the home-cut jobs we observed on classmates were horrendous. Del summed it up in his own succinct style, "Well, at least Father has his eyes open when he clips."

Music in the school curriculum pretty much depended on the talents and inclinations of the individual teacher. Each teacher was supplied with a pitch pipe and after our A was sounded, we would all sing mightily, if off key.

My intermediate grade teacher went beyond the call of duty and aspired to stage a musicale for parents' day. Cousin Gaga and I were invited to try out for a solo part in the production. We went to the teacher's home on a Saturday morning for the audition. Mrs. Thoreson had chosen a song that we sometimes sang in school: "When You and I Were Young, Maggie." She played the piano accompaniment. I gave forth first. My effort was a rather feeble one. "I wandered today to the hill, Maggie, to watch the scenes below." My boyish soprano faltered a bit on the hill and then got out ahead of the music on the downhill scenes. "The creek and the creaking old mill, Maggie, as we used to long, long ago." I managed to cross the creek and then in unfeigned falsetto I out-creaked the old mill. . . . "But to me, you're as fair as you were, Maggie, when you and I were young." I choked a bit on this mushy ending and gladly yielded the stage to Gaga. I had a distinct feeling that Mrs. Thoreson wasn't overly impressed with my singing.

Gaga was in top form that morning. He really belted it out in style. The creaking old mill wheel fairly danced. "What a ham!" I thought. Mrs. Thoreson's effusive praise and Gaga's beaming face left no doubt as to the outcome. For a fleeting moment I felt a tinge of envy, but I was by no means unhappy that Gaga had won the starring role.

Hannaford schoolboys walked circumspectly whenever the awesome figures of Ted Dally and Les Thoraldson loomed ahead in the schoolyard. Ted held undisputed sway as the town bully, with Les his backup man. The uninitiated younger students studiously avoided any kind of confrontation with the browbeating pair. It was my ill fortune to become one of their hapless victims on the morning they were terrorizing early comers by exploding giant caps under their backsides. I elected to try and outrun the tormentors, which placed me at a distinct disadvantage. It seemed that each terrifying explosion under my rear lifted me into the air. It was a mirth-provoking scene for noncombatants, but a highly humiliating experience for me.

Though not of a particularly vengeful nature, I found myself entertaining a distinct longing to turn the tables on these swaggering overlords of the playground. The opportunity came in an unexpected way. Mr. Sorenson, our janitor, became incapacitated, and Father was hired in his place. I occasionally helped Father with some of his cleaning and boiler room duties; this gave me access to rooms in the schoolhouse that before had been off limits. Adjacent to the boiler room was a storeroom of sorts in which football gear was kept. It was also used as a dressing room by the players. Adjoining the storeroom was a science classroom. Within the room a large stuffed pelican, from his place atop a wall cabinet, kept a glassy-eyed surveillance of all who entered. A moth-eaten moose head, a gift from some long-forgotten benefactor or perhaps his long-suffering wife, adorned the rear wall.

Members of Hannaford's football team furnished their own equipment, and the helmets particularly reflected individual tastes and pocketbooks. Each player further individualized his headgear by painting his moniker in a conspicuous place. This made it easy for me to identify Ted's and Les's gear. Even without a name, I'd have recognized Les's helmet. It consisted of a few battered pieces of leather and was almost bereft of any padding. In a game Les used his

Even though our clothing was drab, we all dressed alike.
1924. (Del standing second from left.)

Our Hannaford schoolhouse.

Harvey in high school.

hard head as a battering ram, seemingly unfazed by the knocks on his ill-protected noggin.

I draped Ted's helmet and team jersey over the sagging pelican. Les's gear somehow looked quite natural on the moose's noble head. I was quite pleased with my handiwork, my only regret, that I wouldn't be in that classroom when Ted and Les entered.

Reported results from overheard conversation were all that I had hoped for. For once the shoe was on the other foot. Ted and Les were completely nonplussed. Even the teacher apparently enjoyed their discomfiture. When the class wit wondered aloud what Les was doing up on the wall, the room rocked with laughter. Ted's and Les's scowling faces boded ill for the perpetrator of the trick.

Revenge can be sweet. That night I slept the sleep of the innocent.

Father had no regrets that his schooling had ended with sixth grade. He had learned to read and write and do sums, and in his way of thinking, that was enough. Too much book larnin' could turn a boy's head away from useful pursuits. Father claimed that he knew of a man who could name a horse in five languages and yet was so ignorant that he bought a cow to ride on.

Father also entertained dark doubts about some of the extracurricular knowledge his sons acquired. When he overheard Del relating some questionable worldly notions to Bumpy, Father was heard to complain, "I pay the schoolmaster, but 'tis the schoolboys who educate my son."

I donned my first pair of long dress pants when I started high school in the fall of 1925. The light gray tweed trousers in a mail-order catalog struck my fancy. They had quite wide bottoms, considered very stylish in the mid-1920s. Mother used thrifty foresight in determining my measurements, and that meant the pants would take some growing into. With a powder blue, white-trimmed pullover sweater (also oversized), I cut quite a figure. I felt self-conscious in the new outfit, but with Mother's assurance that I looked very nice ringing in my ears, I made my awkward way to school.

In that gay blue sweater, the loiterers on the playground spotted me coming a block away. As could be expected, Ted and Les were the self-appointed leaders of my reception committee. "Well look at Shorty Long-Pants will ya'," was Ted's derisive greeting. He bowed low before me in mock deference.

Those were fighting words, but discretion overcame valor. Ted and Les were both considerably bigger than I. Besides, I was just too dressed up to fight. Others took up the chant and echoed, "Shorty Long-Pants, look at Shorty Long-Pants!"

The next morning it was a relief to get back into familiar overalls. Several weeks later, upon Mother's prompting, I wore the tweeds and sweater to a school party. I guess time had eased the shock of my appearance, for no one made any untoward comments. The party was planned as a part of freshman initiation, and during the evening I found myself unwittingly involved in a game. The group had been divided, with half receiving a slip of paper containing a question and the rest given an answer to be read. Questions and answers were not matched and some hilarious absurdities were expected.

Either by accident or design, I had been passed by when the slips bearing questions or answers had been distributed. My feelings were not hurt; I counted it somewhat a relief to be an onlooker rather than a participant. It was from this pleasant state of relaxation that I was startled when a teacher, an elderly spinster, approached. "What do you think of me?" she asked. Taken aback, I could only stare in bewilderment. "What do you think of me?" she insisted.

I could feel my ears reddening, and desperation prompted me to blurt, "I think you're old enough to be someone's grandmother." A moment of stunned silence followed before a few suppressed titters broke out.

The unfortunate lady stalked back to her seat stony-faced. I'm certain that she felt victimized, that the answer could only have been a part of something contrived. At the same time, the planners of the game were equally perplexed. How had that answer gotten into their game? As full realization dawned of how my unthinking and unkind words must have cut, I felt very mean and miserable. Should I attempt to apologize and explain my blundering role? Or should I let the poor lady think the worst of those who had organized the game?

Wise and sympathetic Mother helped me out of my dilemma. She encouraged me to face Miss Weatherbee with my story and tell her I was sorry. This I did, and after listening to my halting recital, Miss Weatherbee thanked me graciously. Whether or not she was convinced I was the lone culprit, I felt better about the whole sorry business.

Of the teachers I had in the Hannaford school, one remains etched in my memory above all others. Mr. Eikeland taught classes in mathematics and government in addition to serving as superintendent. He was coldly impersonal, though conscientious and demanding. He dispensed justice and meted out punishment swiftly and with impartiality. One warm spring day I sat in his basement classroom. Several ground-level windows were open. A small boy, enjoying his recess on the playground, ventured to stick his head in an open window and let his spit dribble down the wall. Without pausing in his lecture, Mr. Eikeland walked to the window and summoned the little fellow. Reaching up, he lifted the lad inside and holding him by the seat of his pants, had him wipe the spittle from the wall. That completed, Mr. Eikeland deposited the offender back on the ground outside and with a little slap on the posterior sent him on his way.

I learned a much valued lesson when Mr. Eileland flunked me at the end of a year's study in geometry. Though mathematics was not my best subject, I'm certain I dawdled and did not exert myself in that class. Several times in private conference, Mr. Eikeland warned me that he would fail me in the course if I didn't get down to business. Somehow, I thought he was bluffing. After all, my Father was janitor. Mr. Eikeland wouldn't flunk me. I didn't know Mr. Eikeland very well. He gave me an F in the course, just as he had promised.

Mr. Eikeland was also senior class advisor and coached the senior class play. To my dismay, I found myself a member of the cast for the presentation of "Deacon Dubbs." I felt shanghaied into the role. There were nine members in my class, and Mr. Eikeland had selected a play calling for nine characters. I had a minor part in the play, with my biggest scene as an auctioneer crying an auction sale. A day or two before our one-night performance, I contracted a case of laryngitis. I managed to whisper and rasp my way through dress rehearsal, but by curtain time on show night my voice was completely gone. I nursed a hope that Mr. Eikeland might see fit to make a few alterations and eliminate my part. The old trouper was adamant, however, "The show must go on!"

The show did go on, and in my big scene I could do little but gesture. In my utter frustration, I struggled so hard to get the words out, the audience assumed I was in character—a mute of some kind. The editor of our weekly paper, in his review of our production, stated that I had stolen the show. Mother was unduly proud of her son's fleeting notoriety, while inside, I felt like an impostor. I can only think that Mr. Eikeland must have been mighty relieved that his play directing was over for another year.

High school graduation was a big event to get ready for. Obie had finished high school in 1927, two years ahead of me. I know Father shared Mother's pride in our accomplishment, even though the effort had been with his grudging blessing. An itinerant tailor measured me for a graduation suit. The navy blue serge suiting was chosen by Father for its promised durability. Mother considered it a bit somber for a young man of eighteen but was quite willing to yield to Father's wish in this minor matter. The important thing for Mother was that a second son was getting his high school diploma.

I also had my first haircut in a barbershop. Father and Mother sat behind the row of graduates at the graduation exercises. Mother must have spent most of the evening looking at the back of my head and admiring the haircut, for her only commentary on the evening was, "Harvey had the nicest haircut of any of the boys in the class."

> I turn from the window—here teenagers study and
> perhaps dream,
> Already miles away from the playground's gay abandon.
> Only a few short years ago these also reveled
> In wild shrieking play with scant regard for appearance.
>
> In their impatience to reach adult estate
> There is no looking back to playground's "kid stuff."
> Time seems to them to be dragging its feet.
>
> From our sideline seat it brings never-ending wonderment
> This miracle of growth that is always before us.
> We know it must happen; that it all fits a plan; yet it
> seems
> That only adults lament the briefness of childhood's
> gay years.

—HARVEY SLETTEN, "Childhood's Gay Abandon," 1960

16

Farewell to Bald Hill Creek

TO a young man growing up on Bald Hill Creek, the year 1929 started out brightly enough. I was happily looking forward to graduation from high school in the spring. In the fall I was to enroll at the University of North Dakota. Obie was about to complete a two-year teacher training course and planned to teach in the fall. It was with Obie's encouragement and promise of financial help that I did begin study at the university in September.

In the excitement of starting college, I was scarcely aware of the stock market crash that came in October. Little did freshmen in green beanies or anyone else know that the year 1929 would be remembered as a turning point for America. The 1920s had been a decade of prosperity for most Americans. The depression years were to follow, and our family, like millions of others, was to be greatly affected.

The Reserve Officers Training Corps (ROTC) program at the university was compulsory for all first and second year male students. The coercive feature of the program made it quite distasteful to many students. The student newspaper published derisive commentary on ROTC activities. The World War I uniforms worn by the two-year cadets were dubbed "monkey-suits." Even the instructors, army career officers, were held in low esteem. Perhaps this disrespect for things smacking of the military was characteristic of the postwar decade of the 1920s. The American people were fed up with patriotism and sacrifice and ready to relax.

I accepted the program quite passively. I wasn't overly enthusiastic about donning the ill-fitting uniform and struggling with the wrap-leggings, but I knew it was a part of the game. I entertained no illusions of being the smartest appearing soldier nor the most adept.

The sergeant who drilled us was a career army man and a pretty good guy. He was trying to polish up our "Squads right" and "Squads left," when the paunchy and pompous major stalked in on inspection. Hapless me! I was pivot man in my squad for one maneuver, and, as luck would have it, I goofed. My error headed my squad off in a different direction from the rest of the company. The "Company halt" command brought us to an awkward, out-of-position stop before we could rectify my blunder. The red-necked major strode onto the drill field to confront me. He planted himself squarely in front of me, his potbelly almost pushing me backward. Only the belly kept his jutting jaw out of my face. "Just what does your mother call you?" he sputtered, contempt fairly dripping from every word.

"H-H-H-Harvey, S-S-S-Sir," I stammered.

"Harvey, is it? Well, isn't that nice? How in the world did your mother ever dare let you come up to the university all by yourself?"

I shrank in my oversized uniform as the irate officer proceeded to berate me. Of all the unlikely rookies he had the misfortune to be surrounded with, I was the worst. I was sorely tempted to shove my rifle into his potbelly and make an exit, but I knew that such rash action would have finished me at the university.

I think that my discomfiture was shared in lesser degree by my fellows and by the grizzled sergeant. He had a gruff word of encouragement for me after company dismissal.

The austerity of dormitory living was tempered by an occasional mixer in which men and women students were brought together from their respective dorms for a social event. The matrons of the cooperating halls introduced each young man to a young lady, who became his date for the evening. I think the well-meaning dorm mothers made clumsy attempts to match personalities. My partner for the evening must have found me a very dull fellow. Ill versed in social amenities, I could think of little to say. Most of the other couples mingled freely and exchanged dances. I didn't dance, and the evening had its share of uncomfortable moments for both of us.

After the party I very properly walked the young lady back to her residence hall. We walked in silence, each of us entertaining our own thoughts. At the door I mumbled, "Thanks for a pleasant evening," and stiffly bade her good-night. Needless to say, that romance didn't get off the ground.

Though the university was only ninety miles from Hannaford, I didn't get home until Christmastime. Then I traveled by train, with rail distance from Grand Forks to Hannaford being close to 200 miles and involving an overnight stop at Fargo.

I attended the university only a year and then transferred to Valley City State Teachers College.

The depression only intensified distress and hardship in and around Hannaford. Farmers had been a depressed group ever since the end of World War I. The general prosperity of the 1920s had not reached equally to farmers and workers. Many people were far from rich. Everyone felt the pinch of trying to eke out a living. Farmers stretched their credit to the breaking point, and the people in town, dependent on farm income and spending, found themselves going down along with the farmer.

The Hannaford bank, along with hundreds of others across the country, closed its doors in 1930. At the time, I had a balance in my account of $18.40. The bank went into the hands of receivers, and about a year later depositors were paid off at 10 percent. The $1.84 check I received seemed a cruel affront. Disgruntled depositors muttered darkly against Mr. Wigen. Many were convinced that somehow he had stolen their money. That the bank had been forced under because of defaulted mortgages was uncomprehended by distraught people who had lost their savings. The tormented banker was practically forced into seclusion by unthinking people. Father and Mother expressed deep sympathy for Mr. Wigen and stoutly defended his honesty.

Del finished high school in 1930, just a year behind me. Two of us in college at once was out of the question. Even my continuing for another year of teacher training at times appeared doubtful. There was little for Del in or around Hannaford. Jobs became virtually nonexistent. The most pitiable victims of the depression were the unemployed. It was with this bleak outlook that Del and a high school classmate took to the road.

Infrequent letters from Del revealed but a scanty picture of the miseries and problems faced by the thousands of homeless wanderers. Unwelcomed visitors in one community, they would be given temporary food and shelter and sent on their way. Hitchhiking became more and more difficult as the number of vagrants increased. Much of the time Del and Norman rode freight trains. Occasionally railroad bulls would forcibly remove transients from the trains, but soon the sheer weight of numbers made their task impossible to carry out.

Del and Norman worked whenever and wherever they could

find temporary employment. When they had a few dollars in their pockets they took the fearful risk of being "rolled" by other desperate vagabonds. Del told of slitting open a tube of toothpaste at the bottom end and inserting the tightly rolled currency therein, with the hope that if they were jumped, the cache would be overlooked.

An abashed and conscience-stricken Del described one unhappy incident of their wayworn hoboism. Hungry and penniless, the two had disembarked from a freight train at a tank town in Wyoming. Urgency prompted them to go into a small eating establishment and order a lavish breakast of bacon and eggs. After downing the food, Del and Norman divulged to the lady owner their inability to pay for the meal. The poor woman, almost in tears, lamented, "Did you have to order my best breakfast?" She declined their work offer and sorrowfully indicated that they should leave. She would not call the police.

A dirt-stained Del dropped from the tender of a passenger locomotive just a couple of days before Christmas. Half-frozen, and with face blackened by sooty smoke from the coal burner's stack, Del was scarcely recognizable. Stealing a ride atop the careening tender of a high-wheeler was risky business at any time, and in the dead of winter it was suicidal. Somehow Del had survived. At coaling or watering stops the stowaway would scramble down and conceal himself until the fireman had completed his task and retreated to the locomotive cab. Often the train was moving again before the nonpaying passenger grabbed for a handhold and clawed his way back up the slippery rungs.

As usual we had a happy, if spartan, Christmas. At least the family was together and there was food on the table. It could only have been a bleak holiday season for many. Newspapers were filled with disturbing pictures of soup lines and Hoovervilles. Hopelessness was etched in the faces and manifest in the hunched figures of the shuffling lines.

Del returned to his wanderings soon after the Christmas holidays. He appeared determined not to add to his parents' burden by staying at home. Though it must have grieved both Father and Mother to have Del go, it did mean one less mouth to feed.

Father had always enjoyed perfect health, with little awareness of the sense of his own well-being. I'm sure he gave little thought to his health, and perhaps that in itself kept him well. When he started to complain of stomach pains we were all surprised, though not unduly concerned. He had suffered a rather hard fall from a ladder shortly before, and in his mind and Mother's, that fall seemed related to his mounting discomfort.

When it became apparent that his stomach misery was not going to correct itself, Father yielded to Mother's pleading and went to a medical center at Fargo for a checkup. An exploratory operation revealed cancer of the liver. The disease had spread far enough so that treatment was considered by the examining doctors as hopeless. There was nothing to do but to sew him up and send him home to get his affairs in order.

Father's illness was terminal. I'm not certain that the full import of that pronouncement dawned upon us immediately. We didn't talk about it, but a sense of foreboding pervaded our usually happy home. Father withdrew to himself. He seemed to become his own exclusive object. This was hard for us to understand, as selfishness was totally alien to Father's nature. It was as though a stranger filled the space Father had occupied so lately, in his own and in the family's eye.

Within a matter of weeks Father returned to the hospital. Constant doses of morphine were administered to relieve the acute pain he suffered. I visited Father only once in the hospital and was appalled at his emaciated appearance. He knew the end was near and expressed great concern as to whether Del would come home to see him. In his fevered mind, Father expressed the thought that Del perhaps cared little that his father lay dying. I tried my best to assure Father that Del did care and that he would be home soon. That, however, was not to be. Death came mercifully soon. The bell tolled for Father in the early summer of 1931. During Del's year of wandering, he maintained only infrequent contact with home. This bit of personal tragedy was but an infinitesimal part of the unhappy dislocations of family ties occasioned by the depression of the 1930s.

Mother was made of stern stuff. The warm and kind heart that had nurtured us was also a stout one. In her life, affection and danger were not strangers. Now it was the love and hope for her children that bolstered her courage. Mother's inner strength helped us bear with composure the death of our father.

Our legacy consisted of cherished memories. Mother and Obie, suddenly thrust into man's estate, struggled with unpaid bills. Mother wisely decided to move her family to Valley City, where there was a teachers' college. Tears fell as we followed our meager possessions down the dusty road in the late summer of 1931. We didn't look back.

Harvey in his ROTC "monkey suit."

Father (top left in jacket, hat, and tie) putting on a show for the girls with a few other dare-devils in 1908.

Harvey's first school.

17

The Teacher Burned
Too Much Coal

IN the spring of 1932 I started looking for a teaching job. It proved to be a frustrating experience. I would hear of a vacancy for which I appeared to be qualified, only to find that it had been filled by the time I appeared on the scene. Employed teachers were hanging on to their jobs, even in the face of wage cuts. It was very much an employer's market. School boards could hold out for experience and offer the position to the lowest bidder.

In midsummer I was still searching hopelessly for a position by day and tossing restlessly by night. Any hope of being a successful applicant seemed to lie in a personal interview, so I hitchhiked over much of North Dakota running down leads. Always the answer was, "Sorry, the vacancy has been filled," or "We want an experienced teacher." In my mind I became convinced that I was pursuing a will-o-the-wisp.

On one such quest I found myself stranded in late afternoon in Brantford, North Dakota, a small town far off the beaten track and over a hundred miles from home. It had taken me since early morning to hitchhike to the place and I knew it was highly unlikely that I would get far on the return journey that day. I sadly fingered the fifteen cents remaining in my pocket. While I was considering my quandary, I noticed a commotion at the railroad yard a few blocks away. An eastbound freight train highballing through town had been braked to a shrieking, grinding stop. A happy thought—a way out of my dilemma—suddenly came. That freight train would pass through Hannaford and likely stop to take on coal. I spoke aloud, "Why not hop it?" I could stay the night with friends in Hannaford and hitchhike home to Valley City in the morning. Eagerly I directed my steps toward the waiting train.

As I approached the railroad tracks I was astounded at the number of railroad tramps riding that freight. Every one of the open boxcars revealed men sitting or standing in the doorways, gazing out. Others had disembarked to stretch and stroll. I was used to seeing tramps or hoboes aboard the freight trains that had rumbled through Hannaford, but never in these numbers. I struck up a conversation with a friendly pair. They, along with the rest of the men, were jobless ex-soldiers on their way to Washington to press Congress for an immediate bonus to veterans.

I learned that the train had made the unexpected stop because of an accident. A man had been trying desperately to drive some of his cattle off the track in the face of the approaching freight. At the last moment the panicky animals had turned on him and pushed him almost into the path of the onrushing train. The protruding steam cylinder of the locomotive had struck the unfortunate fellow a glancing blow and hurled his body outward, away from the track. The injured man was put aboard the caboose and the engine uncoupled from the train and backed six miles to New Rockford, a larger town where medical attention was available.

The resultant delay gave me ample time to weigh my decision about boarding the freight train when it resumed its journey. Some of the migrants were rather unsavory-looking characters. I was wearing my much-prized athletic sweater emblazoned with the Valley City Teachers' College emblem, and several of the men were eyeing it in a rather covetous fashion. A lean man wearing a baseball cap offered to buy the sweater. With an uneasy heart I assured him it was not for sale. I had almost changed my mind about hopping the freight when I noticed a loner sitting in the doorway of a car. His clean-shaven face and clear eyes invited confidence. He had noticed the undue interest in my sweater evinced by some of his traveling mates. His name was Jim Marek and he was from Everett, Washington. Jim asked me if I smoked. He needed a cigarette but had no money. I remembered the fifteen cents in my pocket. We were still waiting for the locomotive to return from its mercy run. I made a hurried trip back to the town's only store and purchased a nickel sack of Bull Durham and two candy bars. Jim accepted the tobacco and candy bar with quiet dignity. He had neither asked for nor expected a handout. He rolled the first cigarette with trembling fingers.

The returning locomotive puffed past us to the head of the train of cars. A jolt traveled the length of the train as the coupling was made up front, then we heard the sound of air filling the brake hoses. I was still standing alongside the boxcar and Jim extended his hand in a good-bye gesture. "I'm going along, Jim, give me a hand up." I was barely in when the car pulled forward with a screech of stretched couplings, and we were rumbling on our way.

Jim and I moved away from the doorway to the windless space forward of the doors. A sheet of cardboard was our only cushion from the vibrating floor. Within the confines of the swaying car the wooden walls and roof picked up the clatter of the wheels and amplified it into a general roar. I found it uncomfortable either to sit or stand. The noise limited our talking.

Hour after hour we rumbled on. Darkness fell, and I knew for a certainty that the train had highballed through Hannaford without stopping. Sleep was out of the question, and I steeled myself to endure the rocking, vibrating floor and the reverberating din. Along toward midnight the freight gradually slowed and finally squealed to a halt. Pressure went off the brake hoses with a whoosh. I hadn't the slightest idea where we were, but I knew that I had best disembark. I bade my newly found friend a hasty good-bye and wished him success in Washington. Then I stepped into the darkness and dropped to the cinders.

A light mist was falling. The train had apparently stopped in open country, but I could see faint lights up ahead. I made my stumbling way toward them. As I approached the station, I was able to orient myself by noting the designation on the depot. The freight had stopped at the outskirts of Dilworth, Minnesota, at that time a division point on the Great Northern.

I made my way to the town's only hotel. Perhaps I could spend the rest of the night sitting in the hotel lobby. The night clerk soon bustled over and informed me I couldn't stay there. Once again I hit the street. The light rain continued to fall as I retraced my steps toward the edge of town. A barn loft offered welcomed sanctuary and I wearily curled up in the fragrant hay. I was rudely awakened when someone stumbled over my legs in the darkness. A mumbled, "Sorry, Buddy," made me realize I had company. Some other vagabond had also needed a dry sleeping place.

The next day I hitchhiked back to Valley City. I often thought about Jim Marek, my boxcar partner on that wild midnight ride. The bonus marchers did not fare too well. When Congress adjourned without paying heed to the veterans' demands, a majority of the men gave up and went home, assisted by government loans for train fare. Several thousand stayed on, and after a clash with the police, orders were given to General Douglas MacArthur to use the regular army to restore order. The men were evicted from their camps, their shacks burned to the ground. I wondered if Jim returned to his home in the Evergreen State, if he continued his wanderings, or if he got swallowed up in some big city, as did so many homeless men.

In late summer my efforts were finally rewarded. I was offered a job in a one-room rural school. A teacher had resigned, choosing marriage rather than face another lonely year in Paradise School District.

On a Saturday afternoon in early October 1932, I disembarked from the branch line train at McHenry, North Dakota, a tiny town at the end of the line. I had arranged to board and room with a farm family who lived "tolerably close" to the school where I would teach. I was standing on the depot platform gazing dejectedly at the departing "dinky" train when Hank ambled up.

Seeing I was the only passenger, he came up with an inspired observation, "You must be the new teacher."

"And you must be Henry Johnsgaard."

"Yup." One huge hairy paw wiped a trickle of tobacco juice from a bewhiskered chin and the other crunched the bones in my right hand. "Air yuh riddy?"

Hank led the way to his wagon. Four horses were hitched to a grain tank heaped high with large lumps of lignite coal. Hauling a load of wheat to town, toting home a part of the winter's coal supply, and meeting the new teacher was all in a day's work for Hank. He was a very practical man. He tossed my suitcase to the very top of the load where momentarily it teetered precariously, then wedged itself between two huge chunks of coal. "Climb up," said Hank, "and we'll start fer home."

It turned out to be seven dusty miles to Hank's farm, and the horses plodded along with the heavily loaded wagon.

"Bertha, this is the new teacher." Thus I met the wonderful people with whom I was to live for the next eight months. Their warmth and kindliness more than made up for what they lacked in material comforts.

My bedroom was an attic loft reached by climbing a ladder. Bertha hesitatingly asked if I would mind sharing the bed with Ernest. Ernest was six years old and would be one of my first-grade pupils. He was also to become my pal and confidante. I remember the ponderous horsehide robe that covered us on cold winter nights. The original owner had been a dappled gray. The mane and part of the tail were still attached.

Sunday afternoon I hiked up to my school. The "tolerable distance" turned out to be three-fourths of a mile if I took a short cut through the pasture. The desolate little schoolhouse was perched atop a rock-covered hill amid a treeless expanse of rolling prairie wasteland. A ramshackle barn and two decrepit outhouses completed this rustic campus. A dispirited and lonely young man sat on the schoolhouse steps that evening and watched the autumn sun lower over the bleak hills.

The next morning eighteen assorted youngsters were on hand bright and early to stare with misgivings at the new teacher. Five were first-graders. These I viewed with trepidation. My practice teaching had been in eighth-grade history. How could I teach beginning reading?

Those first days I waited hopefully for the county superintendent to come to my rescue. We were well into the second week when her Model A Ford came chugging up the rocky trail. That dear little gray-haired lady—I could have kissed her! Patiently she guided my faltering efforts with the beginners. When she left at the end of the day she had given me some semblance of confidence. I was not to see her again until spring. She had roughly fifty schools to visit, and snow made mine inaccessible.

I hadn't received my first paycheck when two life insurance agents descended upon me. Things were tough in their line of business too, and even a fifty-dollar-a-month school teacher was considered a live prospect. We left the matter of a modest policy unsettled for the moment, with the understanding that the salesmen would return in a couple of weeks. We stood on the schoolhouse step as the two prepared to depart. They were in an expansive mood. The autumn sun was sinking low over the bleak hills as the spokesman of the two exclaimed, "My you have an inspiring view here!"

I thought to myself, "That fellow has poetry in his soul." I regarded the desolate scene as anything but inspiring.

Two weeks later, to the day, the two insurance men returned. I wasted no time in telling them I was definitely not in the market for life insurance at the moment. Again the scene was the same as they prepared to leave. Both men this time, however, looked a bit down-in-the-mouth. The philosopher of the earlier episode stared again at the forbidding landscape. This time I distinctly overheard him mumble—perhaps to himself, perhaps to his partner—"Man, what a godforsaken place this is!"

As they drove off, I sat down on the steps and laughed until the tears came.

Winter's icy blasts brought new problems. Occasionally some of the pupils were delivered to the door by horse-drawn sleigh. More often than not, pathetic little figures trudged across snow-covered hills. Frostbite was common and sudden blizzards an incessant worry. Parents seemed to have complete faith in God and the teacher, while I, knowing the teacher pretty well, did a lot of praying.

One poignant recollection: the thoughtless lout who upon delivering a load of children proclaimed for all to hear, "Pearl smells like a billy goat." Pearl was fourteen years old; her sobs did not subside until noon. The allegation was not without basis of fact. Saturday night ablutions, starting with the youngest, took place in a wash tub by the stove. By the time six or seven had preceded her, Pearl was asleep, or the hot water had been used up.

Came spring and the bleak prairie hills erupted with gay crocuses. During recess periods we played softball and, at times, perhaps were a little tardy in getting back to lessons.

My first-graders, including Ernest, were reading "tolerably well"—this noted happily by Bertha and Hank. Reluctantly I marked off each passing day.

Hank torpedoed my contentment in his inimitable, brusque fashion. "They don't aim to hire you back fer next year. The board reckons as how yer a fair to middlin' teacher. The young'uns have all learned to read tolerably well, but you've burned just too derned much coal this winter."

A tinge of bitterness crept through shocked disbelief. My school stood on a hill, utterly naked and exposed to frigid winds. The other two schools in the district were partially sheltered by trees and faced south.

Hank knew my thoughts. "That buildin' of your'n is as drafty as longhandled underwear with the trap door down. It always takes some more coal, but nothin' like you burned up."

Seeing my crestfallen countenance, Hank tried to save the day with a dandy, "Well, anyhow, yer the hottest teacher in the whole dern county." His guffaw tapered off abruptly with Bertha's icy glance.

Hank's bombshell echoed in my mind: "A fair to middlin' teacher, but you burned jest too derned much coal." So this was the measuring stick. Stinking lumps of lignite coal counted more than the fact that my beginners could read "tolerably well." I had failed in my first school!

The next few days Hank was away more than usual. I was to

realize later that a seed of suspicion had sprouted in that practical mind of his. With characteristic thoroughness, he launched his own private investigation among the neighbors. It bore fruit.

He tried to be casual as he triumphantly announced, "Well, yer hired back! Seems as how the feller that hauled coal to yer school got a mite light fingered. Part of each load went into his own coal shed at home."

Gone is the one-room school—unwept. Of the children, I can only speculate. Doubtless, somewhere, Pearl revels in the luxury of indoor plumbing. I like to think that Ernest succeeded. He did learn to read "tolerably well."

Epilogue

FATHER might have been unbelieving as to the efficacy of book learning, but I know he would have shared Mother's pride had he lived to see his children grow up. Obie attained a Ph.D. degree and had a distinguished career at a large state university. I earned an M.A. degree in economic education and, after a teaching career, turned to writing. Del became a maintenance electrician at one of the Bureau of Reclamation's large western hydroelectric plants. Irrepressible Bumpy turned out to be the businessman of the family. He has in turn been automobile dealer, business promoter, and real estate broker. Tina and her husband are North Dakota farmers. So far have the children of a public school janitor with a sixth-grade education come.

I mention this with no sense of boasting, but with a deep sense of gratitude that I was born in a country where such upward mobility is not only possible but quite commonplace. Some in our country today (1977) believe that in the long run we may see the virtual end of education as a means of upward mobility in America. I prefer to think that both the need and desire for higher learning can only intensify—that untold possibilities lie ahead. Ours was a modest success story that has been and will be repeated over and over again. Mother had unshakable faith in a greater possibility for her children. For a family growing up on Bald Hill Creek, the pursuit of happiness led upward. The American Dream became our destiny.

> Beautiful, viable, and free—
> America partly is, and wholly hopes to be.

—HARVEY SLETTEN, 1976